A Common Sense Approach to Dressing for the Workplace

DRESS
TO IMPRESS

How a Navy Blazer Changed My Life!

❧❧❧

by
Joyce Nelson Shellhart
founder of *Ready For Success*

BOOK PEDDLERS • MINNETONKA, MN

cover designer: Dianne Silverman
editor: Abby H. Rabinovitz
illustrator: lana k. beck

ISBN 1-931863-09-1
Copyright © 2005 Joyce Nelson Shellhart

BOOK PEDDLERS
15245 Minnetonka Blvd •Minnetonka, MN 55345
952-912-0036
www.bookpeddlers.com

printed in China

04 05 06 07 08   5 4   3   2

Acknowledgements

❧

Trinity Episcopal Church, Excelsior, MN gave us our roots, Episcopal Community Services gave us our trunk of support, but the volunteers of *Ready for Success* are the sunshine and gentle showers that nourished our clients with their amazing gifts.

Information regarding the *Ready for Success* program at Episcopal Community Services is included with the consent of Episcopal Community Services.

My dear husband Bruce Nelson *(I did a much better job of choosing this time round)* and our children, Stephanie and Jack, Christopher and Michelle, Margaret, Kati, Sarah and Anne, and our grandchildren who add so much fun in our lives, Kiley Lyn and Jack Thomas. Thank you Marv and Helen, my in-laws, for your faith in me. Thank you mom—Edna Winsor—for working so hard to keep our family together in difficult times.

Friends and family who have supported, encouraged, and believed in me while I have traveled this road, especially Sue, Joyce, Gretchen, Jan, Donna, Lorna, Andrew, the Kathys and so many others that should be listed here. Thank you Vicki and your staff for believing that this book was really important and needed to be done.

How A Navy Blue Blazer Changed My Life!

❦

Once upon a time, there was a young woman in college.

She met a young man. On that first night he told her he would marry her. She laughed and replied, "No way," but she was intrigued and flattered.

A few months passed. He became her constant companion.

He liked to drink, but it was college and who didn't?

He would get a little jealous, well maybe a lot jealous. But that only meant he loved her.

He wanted to know her every move when he wasn't around. After a while she was careful whom she would mention she had seen at study group or for coffee after class. But that only meant he loved her.

They married two weeks after she graduated from college.

In a few years they had their first daughter.

He still drank quite a bit. She had quit; she didn't really enjoy drinking and the fights that would erupt.

He had become even more jealous, suspicious, and criticized her constantly. But he only said and did those things because he loved her and he wanted to help her.

The years passed, she tried hard not to evoke his wrath. After all, it was always her fault if he got mad and put his fist through the door.

One day he poked his finger so hard into her chest while yelling at her, it left bruises for days. But he was sorry afterwards.

He told her it was her fault for making him so mad, and she accepted what he said as truth.

The next time he pushed her down. He claimed she was so clumsy that she tripped. How could anyone that stupid be so clumsy too?

He loved her and was only trying to help her.

She never dressed up. If she did, he would question how could she spend money on herself? Who was she trying to impress? Did she have a new boyfriend?

One day he was yelling at their teenage daughter. His accusations about her behavior, her clothing, and her friends sounded too familiar—and unacceptable—

...and that was the day she woke up.

❦❦❦❦

I was blessed to have had many friends and family support me through this difficult time. It is hard to face the truth about one's life, especially in a relationship of 20 years. It is even more difficult for your children, especially teenage daughters, facing their own choices in relationships and their futures. Their future was the biggest reason I made the choices I did. I know personally how choices repeat themselves in families, and I wanted more for my daughters. I realized I had married a man just like my stepfather. I had hated it when he had said the same sort of things to me, yet here I was, allowing my husband, the father of my child, to say those same things to her. And she believing it must be OK, she had heard him say those things to me. It had to stop and it had to stop now!

During the process of removing my husband's negative influence from my life, *(I used to call him the jerk, now I refer to him as the negative influence)*, I decided I wanted to present myself differently to the world. I had been a jeans and t-shirt kind of gal. I had been a high school art teacher. Every year on my annual evaluation I received one negative comment, DOES NOT DRESS APPROPRIATELY FOR THE JOB.

I began observing my friends in church. What did they wear that helped them create an appearance of success and confidence? I decided I needed a navy blue blazer. I was in the process of a divorce, concerned about losing my home, had a small disability income and certainly couldn't afford a new blazer. Besides, my teenage daughters needed things more. I began searching Goodwill and thrift shops for an inexpensive "gently used" navy blue blazer. I am a size 20-22 and finding something to fit me that wasn't worn out or clown-like was a real challenge. I finally found my *Navy Blue Blazer*. I put it on over the same jeans and t-shirt that the week before I had worn to my women's group at church.

"Joyce, did you cut your hair?"

"Did you lose weight?"

"You look great!"

The only thing different was the navy blazer. After years of negative comments, I needed those positive comments. I wanted more of this positive stuff; it was like a drug to my soul.

Making the change was not easy. Fortunately my friends were supportive. However, my children repeated the same questions their father had asked.

"Who you trying to impress?"

"Who do you think you are?"

I remember slipping on the navy blue blazer to go to a high school conference for my youngest daughter, then a freshman, "You're going like that! Who do you think you are?" Fast forward four years, and I'm going to a school conference for my now senior daughter. I put on a nice pair of khakis and a sweater. Her question now is, "You're going like that?" She now expected to see me present myself in an even more professional manner.

I remember trying out a scarf around my neck for the first time—tying it and retying it for twenty minutes. I walked out of the bathroom. My daughters began laughing and saying, "Who are you trying to impress?" I just put my shoulders back and walked out the door. I knew then who I needed to impress.

MYSELF

Table of Contents

introduction

The fact is people do treat you as they perceive you to be. That perception has a lot to do with what you look like and how you present yourself.

I have met some amazing women on my journey. Many people have shared their personal stories with me—stories that have brought tears to my eyes, and yet to see them today, to know the struggles they have encountered to learn to present themselves in a whole new light, is awe-inspiring. I don't claim to know everything there is to know in personal presentation, but I am here to share what I've learned. In fact, if you have lunch with me, you may be amazed to discover that when I am talking, I put my elbows on the table, I lean in and listen with my full being. This is a habit I have tried many times to break, but one I have learned to accept and actually like about myself.

My mother was a widow, working in a factory to support five children in the 1960s and 1970s. In her young adult life she had actually done some modeling. However the need to put food on the table for hungry children forced her to seek a more stable occupation. Most of my youth she wore jeans, t-shirts and heavy shoes to work. She sewed much of her non-work clothing as well as ours. I remember being embarrassed by my hand-sewn clothing, and hand-me-downs from family friends. Eventually clothing became something I felt I wasn't very good at selecting. When I married, and my *"wasband" (I am referring to my former husband—its shorter and more to the point than the "ex-husband" term)* questioned my clothing choices, my confidence in my personal selection became even more uncertain.

So how did I begin to change my personal appearance? I purchased a "gently used" navy blue blazer and I:

- threw it on over jeans and a t-shirt.
- wore it with a pair of khakis and a turtleneck.
- folded a large square scarf in a triangle, draped it around my shoulders over the blazer; laid the ends under the lapel, and put it on over a simple skirt, slacks or blouse.
- draped a large square scarf folded in a triangle under the blazer, crossed over and tucked the ends under my bra, put the blazer on over the scarf, and buttoned the blazer. The scarf acted as a blouse effect.
- tied a small square scarf around my throat and experimented with it off to one side or in the middle when wearing jeans and a t-shirt.
- put it on over a 2-piece dress.

If the dress was something very different from navy blue, like red, I put on a long scarf, draped it under the lapel with navy and red to 'tie' the look together.

My first step was to choose a base color—navy blue. It was a beginning for me. I searched garage sales, estate sales, and clearance racks for very low-cost accents to go with navy blue, such as scarves, jewelry, lapel pins, turtlenecks, blouses, shoes and handbags. In a matter of months I had built an entire wardrobe around one color—and basically one item of clothing. Needless to say I quickly wore out that blazer. Now I felt more self-assured about what I wanted, so when my sister asked what I would like for my birthday I confidently replied...*a new navy blue blazer!*

I am an inch taller today, and to be honest, women in my age group don't normally grow one inch. I suspect I only stand taller with more confidence and self-assurance. Knowing you are dressed appropriately for any situation, allows you to concentrate on other things, such as conversation, work, and being in the moment.

In the Beginning

In December of 1996, while channel surfing, *(I had gotten custody of the remote and the recliner in the divorce)* I happened across a short piece on a TV news magazine about the *Bottomless Closets* in Chicago. They provided clothing for low-income women for interviews. I awoke the next morning and sat down at a used computer recently given to me by a friend. I wrote a business plan for what such an organization would need to begin. I had no previous experience in business or the non-profit world, other than as a volunteer and client. I was on disability from teaching due to Multiple Sclerosis and in the midst of an ugly divorce. In hindsight it is no wonder people would sometimes look at me with amazement when I was so clear and articulate about what the organization should look like. I knew from my personal experience that there was a need—not only for the clothing—but also for guidance.

In 1997, a group of volunteers and myself from Trinity Episcopal Church in Excelsior, Minnesota formed *Ready for Success*. We opened our doors in November 1997 in the parish hall. We began as an outreach project of our church. Most of our early volunteers were members of the church and their friends. We were open 4 days a month, by appointment only, and seeing clients only upon referral.

Ready for Success was formed to provide low-income women in the Minneapolis/St. Paul area with a free clothing resource for interviews and the workplace. We provided more than just clothing for these women. Each woman received the personal attention of a volunteer personal shopper who helped the woman "shop the racks" of our gently used clothing. The two would spend about two hours "shopping" for four outfits including shoes, handbag, bras, underwear, scarves and jewelry—items she needed for her personal situation. In the winter, if we were lucky, we'd even find her a coat. These women were invited to return for an additional two visits—though we encouraged her to save one appointment for another season—as helping them develop a four-season wardrobe was necessary in Minnesota. During the "shopping trip" many ideas, tips and suggestions were shared between the shopper and her personal volunteer about entering the workplace.

The women who come to *Ready for Success* are accepted by referral-only from over 50 social service agencies throughout the Minneapolis/St. Paul metro area. These include: battered women shelters, welfare-to-work programs, recovery programs, ex-offender programs, refugee programs, job skills and work readiness programs, dislocated worker programs, and displaced-homemaker programs.

The Success of *Ready for Success*

- In 1999, due to construction at our church, we moved to a larger space in Minnetonka, Minnesota, and were able to be open additional hours. Our volunteer base grew beyond our parish community.
- In 2001 we joined Episcopal Community Services, a statewide social service organization offering us more opportunities for expansion and support.
- In January of 2003, we opened a second site on the east side of St. Paul, at Hazel Park Congregational Church.
- In 2003 we had over 1000 client appointments, which equates to nearly 100,000 pieces of clothing and undergarments passing through our doors.
- In 2003 nearly 200 volunteers served our clients as: personal shoppers and clothing inventory specialists. These people, plus ECS board members and support personnel, donated hundreds of hours.

When we first opened, I was constantly asked whether or not there was really a need for a service such as this with the influence of "business casual" dress in the workplace. I think our growth and numbers answer that question very clearly—*YES!* As the pendulum has swung from "business casual" to a more professional dress today, the answer is an even more resounding—*YES!*

I have been blessed to know and work with wonderful women at *Ready for Success.* By keeping my eyes and ears open I learned a lot. It was enlightening for me to discover women who I thought always looked so confident and "put together" still obsessed about whether what they were wearing was appropriate. Most relaxed over time as they learn and accept that their personal choices are in line with what other women will be wearing at work, or to the event they are attending. How did they learn that? By watching, talking and sharing with other women. This is what our concept of women helping other women is all about.

Women are always struggling with what is appropriate to wear in a given situation, especially:

- Low-income women, who may know how to dress but can't afford it.
- Women moving from very casual work environments (convenience stores, factories etc.) to office settings.
- Women lacking experience and confidence in this area who are competing with others who have more "dressing for work" experience.
- Women coming from college and training programs where the dress attire was jeans and t-shirts.
- Women looking to change their self-image as well as their entire life.

The last situation is the most profound change a woman can make and the most amazing to witness. Those of us at *Ready for Success* have been truly blessed to be part of the changes made by the women we work with. I am not claiming that an improved wardrobe and personal presentation will get you a job you are not qualified for, help you keep a job you are late to, or get the promotion you don't deserve. Presenting yourself in a professional manner will do those things—in combination with skill, desire and a positive attitude. *And that I know from personal experience.*

This book grew out of an idea to put together the things we shared at *Ready for Success* that could serve as a reference for the women who came to us but also for others who need this information about dressing for the workplace. Eventually, after speaking to groups of potential clients, potential funders, and clothing donors, people would come up to me afterward and say:

- "I wish someone would talk to my entry level employees about how they dress!"
- "I wish someone would talk to my daughter, who is just getting started in the workplace about how she dresses!"
- "I wish I could get my clients going into the 'bank skills' training program to see how important it is to dress the part!"

Many women I worked with found clothing choices as a way to rebel against parents or mothers who did dress very well. Others did not have a role model of a working professional woman to emulate. Still others use "business casual" as a way to avoid worrying about their appearance. Many of them have confided in me that they do wish they knew how to present themselves better and with more confidence.

So here it is—a book with some things your mother probably told you but you weren't listening; some things your mother didn't know and maybe you want to share with her; and some new things to help you get the positive encouragement we all need.

If someone has left this book lying on your desk, don't take offense. They must feel you are worth the effort and may be trying to tell you that your personal appearance is holding you back from reaching new levels of success. If this book is a gift, say thank you, for the giver believes you are capable of much more and just knowing someone believes in us can be a powerful force in our lives.

— Joyce Nelson Shellhart

❧ ❧ ❧

Chapter One

Developing a Sense of Style

ورأورأورأ

Developing a sense of clothing style does not have to involve hours of study or years of experience. Pick any up-scale business-area mall. Sit down on a bench. Grab a cup of coffee and people watch around lunchtime by yourself. I suggest a business area shopping mall preferably with eating establishments and close to an upscale restaurant. The regular suburban shopping mall will not provide the inspiration for the needs of a working wardrobe. I am talking about the kinds of places where women in business grab a quick lunch, meet clients or one another for lunch, or do a little shopping. The movie, *Working Girl,* with Melanie Griffith from the 1980's demonstrates the dress code difference between entry-level employees and executive women even today. I am here to say you don't have to spend a fortune to dress on the level you aspire to, nor is it that difficult. Now, when I comment on someone's outfit as they pass by us in the mall, my daughters laugh at me, "Who are you, the Clothing Police?" What women impress you as successful and why?

Fashion and Style

Remember there is a difference between style and fashion. Fashion changes constantly with each new season and trend. Style is long lasting. A wardrobe based on style will have classic pieces that will carry over from year to year, perhaps with a dash of new colors and accessories. One of the biggest mistakes I see young women and women seeking entry-level positions make is the desire for the latest fashion trend. Their wardrobes quickly become dated. And remember, many of those fashions are designed for tall willowy figures, not the average American figure.

You CAN Shop When You Can't Buy

Stroll through quality department stores, touching fabrics and observing the clothing selections. This research expedition is best done by yourself, without children or friends. It is too easy to become distracted. Avoid the junior, beach, golf wear and exercise wear departments. One of the things my clients tell me most often, is they never go in expensive department stores they can't afford; the clerks act mean, or avoid them. Change your mind set!

Success Secret #1
Shopping and spending are two different activities.
Your bank account is not checked before
you walk in the door of any store.

Yes, you will be treated better and with more respect, if you are clean and neat. Look directly at the clerk and smile "No thanks" when asked if you need any help. I freely admit that my very best bargains have been found in the very best stores. There are still departments and stores I can't afford even 80% off the original price but finding the occasional Ralph Lauren khakis or Tribal black pants for $8.00 is worth the search!

If nothing else, the bathrooms are usually cleaner and less crowded in these up-scale stores. I found my favorite department store because I needed a bathroom. I was so impressed by its upkeep and furnishings that I stopped by the women's department and checked out a small sale sign. The prices in my sizes were amazing! I was hooked!

Fashion Fatalities

Places to avoid business-clothing advice are most fashion magazines. Remember they are there to sell the latest fashion—not help you move up in your career. The other places not to be taken in by are any TV shows geared to the younger crowd. I once had a client tell me she had been sent home from work for wearing a mini skirt. No one had ever told her not to, and she had seen her favorite actress playing the part of a young attorney wearing one.

Look Around

Who impresses you where you work? I encourage women to dress like the women in leadership positions at their workplace. Who signs the paycheck? Who gives the promotions?

Watch people at social functions or your house of worship. What are people wearing that doesn't impress you and why? What clothing outfits seem to say success?

Pay attention to what women are wearing in various businesses. What does the bank teller at your local bank wear? Is it any different from what the loan officer is wearing? What about the customer service representative at the local high-end department store? What is the receptionist wearing at the city office or county office? Most important of all, does what they are wearing say success? Sometimes we can learn more from what NOT to wear, rather than what TO wear.

Success Secret #2

Sometimes our closest family and friends have the most trouble with our new look. We no longer fit their image of us. Ask yourself, who do you need to impress? Start with yourself. *(Yes, you matter!)*

Chapter Two

It's a Work Uniform!

៩▲៩▲៩▲

"Business casual" has changed the look of the American workforce. It has allowed the employee to come to work, in some businesses, quite literally in almost anything they please. It has opened the doors to more choices in clothing for the workplace. Some of those choices are good and some are not so very good. The dress code, written and unwritten, can vary so dramatically from business to business even from department to department. After you have your job, you should look around.

- How do other employees dress?
- How does management dress?
- Are there certain days when better dress is required?
- How casual is "Casual Friday"?

Who is Your Employer?

While "business casual" may be a boom for the employees, I have heard a number of upper level management and customers mourn the loss of professional business attire. When clients tell me they no longer need suits or even blazers for their prospective jobs, I ask them several questions:

- Is the company owned or run by someone under 40?
    If so, it is possibly a very casual atmosphere.

- Is the business in the creative field such as public relations, advertising, or graphics?
    If so, it is possibly more casual with a side of creativity and fun.

- Is the business in the financial field?
    If so, it is probably more conservative.

- Does someone on the East Coast own the company, or is a major stockholder of the business?
    If so, color choices are more limited to black and white, and neutral.

- Does someone on the West Coast own the company, or is a major stockholder of the business?
    If so, it may have a very casual atmosphere.

- Does someone in mid-America own the company, or is a major stockholder of the business?
    If so, this is mainstream America, and will blend both coastal regions.

- Does someone from Europe own the business or is a major stockholder of the company?
    If so, they usually have a higher expectation of clothing quality and conservative dress.

- Is the business located in the suburbs, the city or rural America?
    If so, the more conservative dress is usually found in populated areas. It is interesting to note that the public in some small towns is less accepting of very casual dress in their banks and white-collar businesses.

A company's customer can be very uncomfortable with the way an employee presents herself—and how the company is represented by their employee—it can have a negative effect on the bottom line of the business.

Frequently I'll have a woman look at me blankly, and say, "I don't know. I haven't thought about it." AND that is exactly my point. Limiting yourself to what YOUR idea of "business casual," limits your choices and often your opportunities.

Business Casual

"Business casual" today can vary from jeans with flannel shirts in the winter and t-shirts in the summer to men in suits who don't wear ties on Fridays. The work uniform of the last several decades of the working woman has changed considerably. I remind my clients that in some form it still exists, although often unwritten.

Success Secret #3
Just as you would not consider wearing your McDonald's uniform out on a date, the clothes you wear to work are not what you will probably wear out with your friends or around the house. It is what you need to gain positive strokes at work.

You may not need a suit everyday for work but there are those special occasions—maybe a prospective new customer or an out-of-town buyer is coming into the office. Or there is the BIG meeting. You do need to know how to put on something more professional and feel confident and comfortable in what you are wearing.

Changes in Workplace Attire

CLOTHING CHOICE	*Pre-"Business Casual"*	*Post-"Business Casual"*
SUITS	Dark colors, blazer with skirt or pants of same fabric	Almost any color goes, with some wonderful new easy care fabrics.
TOPS & BLOUSES	Light neutral colors usually silk, rayon, cotton or polyester	Cotton t-shirts or turtle necks worn under blazers, or almost any color silk or great new easy care man-made fabrics for blouses. Beautiful tailored blouses are also now worn open over t-shirt or tank *(not too revealing tank)* as a blazer effect.
SKIRTS	Knee–length or slightly longer, never jean fabric or floor/ankle length	Wide variety of choices, avoiding mini-length and slits to mid-thigh or above.

PANTS	Dark, usually pleated fronts	Khakis and a wide variety of pant choices and lengths, avoiding shorts, capris and blue jeans.
BLAZERS	Structured shoulder pads, length reaching upper thigh or fingertip length with arms placed at side	This is wide open, such as unstructured with softer fabrics, short bolero length to almost knee length, wide variety of lapel or no-lapel choices.

Says Who?

When I began dressing more professionally several years ago, I heard several things that I accepted as fact. I have since discovered that the following can be ignored or overlooked when dressing for the workplace on a tight budget.

Blazer and pants or skirts must always be the same fabric.

Manufactures tell us that. Why? So we buy more. I have had salesclerks tell me I have to buy the matching skirt even though the blazer is the only piece on sale, and to be honest, the only piece I want. I do have a little rule of thumb. Wear the heavier fabric on the bottom as our sense of proportion will accept that better.

Beware of matching blacks and matching navy blues.

This is true, but not to the extent some fashion experts will tell you. Again if the colors are close, I prefer the darker on the bottom, as the eye accepts this as a nicer look. I carry my selection from the closet to the window to double check how close in color they are, or if the colors don't work at all. I have also encountered what one of the volunteers calls the "black navy" or very dark, nearly black. This is a difficult color to match accurately but to be honest one that carries off in public with either black or navy very well.

Your Basic Working Wardrobe

What to Look For

• Pants and skirts in several weights and lengths in your base color. Walk through the department stores and malls to see what the current lengths are in fashion, and think about what you can do to modify skirts and pants, usually hemming is the easiest.

• Blazers, cardigans, and long sleeve tailored blouses that either are in your base color, or complement your base color.

• Tops in your base color to create the two-color outfit or three-color outfit, and tops to complement your base color.

• Belts, shoes and handbags in the base color.

This becomes the basis for your working wardrobe. Keeping to these simple choices in the beginning will simplify your shopping time, make the most out of your closet space, and make getting dressed for work much easier and less stressful.

> ## Success Secret #4
> Choose a base color to work with. Black is probably the easiest and looks great on most women. *(In hindsight I should have chosen black over navy blue, when I began.)*

Acquiring the Basics

It's not rocket science. Follow these ideas and you're in business!

Pants

A basic pair of pants—black pants—is a good place to start. Pleated fronts are slightly dressier than flat fronts. If the pleats pull or open when you are just standing there, move up a size. Or check to see if the button could be moved over slightly to decrease the pressure around your waist. I have worked with women who will pull at the extra fabric in the front on pleated pants, complaining it feels, "funny." No, pleated dress pants don't feel like jeans. They should have a looser feel, with more fabric that nicely lies across your tummy area. Find a second pair of pants to complement the base color.

Pants containing a small amount of spandex have a lot more give and can be very comfortable. I am not talking about spandex leggings for the office. This is exercise wear. In your office khakis or Dockers may be the standard pant of choice. They do come in some great colors, including black. Even if khakis are the office norm, you still need to have a nice pair of pants. They can still make that "career casual" impression.

Skirts

A basic skirt in the same color as your pants should be in your wardrobe. Skirts can be tricky when figuring out the front from the back. Normally the label goes in the back, but occasionally it's on the side. If there is a slit, it should open no higher than slightly above your knee. Try sitting down in front of a three-way mirror if you question this advice. That image will usually convince anyone I've worked with. You can lightly baste the slit closed to the knee then open it later for datewear. Frequently slits or pleats are tacked shut on the bottom of a new skirt. It is okay to open them. Skirts can be knee-length or slightly below, mid–calf length or ankle length. I find skirts that hit across the heaviest part of your calf very unflattering. Either shorten them to the narrowing just above or lengthen to just below the widest part of the calf for a nicer look. Thin straight skirts generally give a slimming look. Full skirts and pleats are always around in some form, but are a more casual look. The pleated skirt with the blazer has made a return in the office, but never a pleated mini skirt. In northern climates, tights with skirts are a good choice in the winter.

Jackets

A blazer in your base color and a second jacket in a complementary or neutral color are a terrific base. Blazers or jackets have a wide range of styles and quality, thanks to business casual. If the pockets are sewn shut, leave them that way. It will prevent you from shoving your hands, keys and other things in them, keeping the jacket looking nice longer without sagging pockets. Clip the threads to open the back pleat if it is sewn shut on a new jacket. Try on a wide variety of blazer lengths. This is easy to do on your research trip through a fine department store. When you see one at a thrift store or garage sale you will already have some idea of the length and the style you are looking for. The long knee-length, the short bolero or the mid thigh length are all suitable choices depending on your body type and comfort level. Are the sleeves too long? Hem them or roll them up. If they are too short, roll them to a ¾ length. I especially like rolled blazer sleeves if there is a nice satin lining. I have a tendency to push blazer sleeves up when I am working any way. Remember a blazer will feel more confining than a t-shirt or sweatshirt. Women will frequently pull their arms and shoulders in unnatural positions showing just how tight the fabric feels. How often in your job do you reach above your head? A blazer two sizes too big creates a sloppy appearance. A properly fitting suit does feel different than t-shirt and sweats but with practice and a little time it will feel less strange and more natural.

double breasted jacket
finger-tip length

single breasted
jacket
knee-length

bolero style

Tops

These four types of tops will carry your outfits through many changes:

- a plain no-pocket solid color t-shirt
- a solid color tank top
- a solid color short sleeve shell
- a solid color tailored button-front blouse

The tailored button-front blouse can also be worn unbuttoned over another top to create a casual layered effect. You may want to remove the shoulder pads in your blouses if you frequently wear them under a jacket with shoulder pads. Velcro is great for offering the versatility of in and out shoulder pads.

I suggest solid color tops in the beginning to help you create that classic "style" look. Prints can range from very casual to very formal, and are pieces you will want to add later. If you can find a simple print which includes your base color and is a complementary color with your second blazer or pant, it will be worth the investment.

Accessories

Shoes in your base color, along with a handbag, trouser socks and nylons will complete any outfit.

Subtle Differences

Dressing appropriately for any situation is really the key to dressing successfully.

Try dressing up khakis and a plain t-shirt: wear a vest, add a scarf, add jewelry—a necklace or pin—tuck in the t-shirt and wear a belt, or add a cardigan, a turtleneck or blazer for another look.

Try dressing down a suit by separating pieces and adding a complementary color jacket or pant. Wear a plain, no-pocket t-shirt under the blazer and a casual shoe.

Women will tell me they don't need a suit but with just a few changes, look at all the great looks they are missing out on. Your look will be:

- *More conservative* which relates to more professional dress when worn with a silk or silk-like blouse either in a pastel, white or off-white. Your shoes should be a solid color pump in a matching color.
- *More relaxed* when worn with a plain solid-color cotton shirt in a complementary color, and even more casual if the t-shirt is striped. Add a shoe with casual accents—a chain, tassels etc.
- *More casual* when the jacket sleeves are rolled to 3/4 length (*in this case wear a short sleeve top underneath and unroll the sleeves when you hang the jacket back up in your closet to prevent permanent creases*),
    a) or put the jacket on with a light pair of khakis, t-shirt or white cotton blouse
    b) or wear the pants with a tucked in t-shirt, put on a scarf
    c) or add a vest or cardigan.

Success Secret #5

How can you sell yourself, if you don't think you have anything to sell? You are worth this opportunity. Repeat this to yourself as often as is necessary.

Dressing for the Interview

Choose your outfit at least one or two steps above the job you are seeking. I tell women to wear the outfit they intend on wearing to the interview around the house first, or out to a mall. Walk around. Get the feel of it. Is it gapping or pulling? Practice sitting down as well as walking up and down stairs. It is better to discover that your blouse becomes too revealing when you move around a couple days prior to your interview rather than during the interview. Remember you want to be able to concentrate on the interview and answering the questions rather than thinking about or obsessing about the fact that your skirt keeps sliding up to an uncomfortable length.

Dressing for the Job

A woman from a bank-skills training program came into *Ready for Success*. She was uncertain whether she even wanted a blazer. We convinced her to try on a lovely Jones of New York suit— just for fun. She turned around to face us after seeing herself in the three-way mirror, with the most amazed look on her face. "I really do look like a bank teller!" Until that moment, I don't think she saw herself mentally in the position she was training for. We laughed and said, "You look like a loan officer or even vice president of the bank!" And suddenly a world of opportunities opened before her eyes.

Research has shown that workers are more productive when dressed appropriately for their job. Especially in the beginning, you want to feel confident and capable of doing your job.

Success Secret #6

Almost everyone who has ever accepted a job or promotion thinks, *"This is over my head and sooner or later they will find out that I don't really know what I am doing."* Never let fear stop you from taking on a new challenge.

You want to look mature, responsible and capable of handling the job, especially in the mirror. So put your shoulders back and believe you can do it because in no time you will be doing it. I have discovered dressing the part goes along with acting the part to develop the confidence needed to fill the part. I have seen this with many women at *Ready for Success* as well as with myself.

Other employees may comment that you "over dress" but that is usually because by your "dressing up" you have set a higher standard for everyone in the office.

You don't need to wear a suit everyday to look professional if your office does not demand it.

Chapter Three

Daywear versus Datewear

ॐॐॐॐ

I peered into the window at the bank drive up. The young woman about to take my deposit tugged at the thin strap of her top. She obviously was not wearing a bra. *"Well, at least she had straps holding up her top this week. Last week it was only a tube top with no straps,"* I thought to myself. The bank teller made me a little nervous taking my deposit. She looked as though she needed the money more than I did.

Later that day, a tall, young, beautiful size 8 woman and I had just finished selecting her work wardrobe when we stepped into the final room for selections—the miscellaneous collection. This room is the "fun" stuff— short outfits, even gowns at holiday time. She grabbed a cute little black leather mini skirt off the rack in her size. "This would be just perfect for the concert I am going to next week. I'll borrow my sister's leather boots. I am going to look so hot!" I laughed and replied, "Great, but don't wear it to work!" She stopped and with all seriousness said, "I know. I was sent home from work last week for wearing a mini skirt. No one had ever told me not to wear a mini skirt to work. I see them do it on TV." This woman had learned a valuable lesson but unfortunately the hard way.

Too Sexy

Dressing "too sexy" is the biggest mistake I see young women make who lack the experience of dressing for the workplace. Whether the skirt is too tight, too short, slit too high, a strappy little sandal with a four-inch heel, revealing tops or lingerie, it is suggestive outwear. Those outfits will get you noticed but will it be the positive type of notice you desire for advancement? Unfortunately not all workplaces will honestly discuss what they expect their employees to wear. You may see other employees dressing this way yet no one will comment directly to you about your similar clothing selections, but rest assured, someone is noticing. It may come up behind your back, during layoff reviews, or when being considered for advancement. Remember you are representing that employer and the company. An employer has the right to expect a certain appearance from their employees. Women are frequently surprised by their own "aha!" moment when I mention this fact to them.

Success Secret #7

Dress for your workplace. You are representing your employer by how you dress and present yourself—not your eligibility on the dating circuit.

Some basic outfits, with a few modifications, can very easily take you from the office to an evening out. Changing from a 2-inch black pump to a strappy black sandal, adding a small evening purse, changing to fun glittery jewelry, and adding a bit more make-up can create a new look for an after work date or event.

Love in the Workplace

A very good friend of mine has had a long career at a large, well-known corporation. She vowed in the very beginning of her career not to date anyone at work. She has had plenty of opportunity but the negatives far out weighed the positives. Many employers have rules against dating in the workplace. Experience has shown that when personal and emotional issues erupt in the workplace (as they sometimes do between two people who are dating) the whole work environment suffers. The issues that may arise if one of the employees is supervising another are even more catastrophic. If you are dressing to impress a particular someone at work or seeking a possible mate from your workplace, think again. Dress to be seen as a confident, hardworking, responsible, capable employee for the people who give the promotions and the raises. Do your dating and mate selections outside the workplace.

If you are single, think about the type of man you would like to attract. How you present yourself, even on the dating scene, sends signals you may or may not want to send. Where do you want to be in 5 years or 10 years and with whom? Are you currently dating a caring, confident, capable, responsible person on the road to a successful life? Do you attract that type of person? If you don't, what can you do to change your dating image? Change the way you dress!

CLOTHING TYPE	*Datewear image*	*Daywear image*
BLOUSES & TOPS	Very low cut either scoop neck, v-neck or unbuttoned to breast	No cleavage exposure

	Too tight, gapping buttons	Proper size perhaps with a minimizer bra
	Animal prints, logos or slogans	Animal prints worn under blazer, just peeking out
	See-through	See-through with proper camisole or under-blouse
	Tube tops	May be worn as strapless bra under clothing
	Tank tops with spaghetti straps or built-in bras	May be worn under unbuttoned blouse or jacket, be careful it is not too tight, with no cleavage showing and don't remove the jacket during work hours.
SKIRTS & DRESSES	Slit above the knee to mid thigh or higher	Slit to knee
	Mini skirt	No shorter than the width of a credit card above the knee *(the narrow width)* when kneeling on the floor.

	Tight, every bulge and muscle shows	Try sitting down, can you do it comfortably? Ask someone you trust to give you an honest opinion. How does it look from the back?
ACCESSORIES	Large earrings that dangle below your chin line.	Simplify your accessory choices
SHOES	Open toes	See chapter on shoes
	Glittering gold and silver colors	Basic neutral colors to match your outfit, preferably your pants or skirt
	4 inch heels	3 inches or under
MAKE-UP	Strong blush, bright lipsticks, heavy eye shadows, colored mascaras	Brown or black mascara, colors of lipstick leaning to naturals tones
HAIR	Dramatic hairstyles, or long hair, dyed unnatural colors	Clean, pulled away from face, especially if long, and always nicely trimmed

Chapter Four

Accessories: Friend or Foe?

Even in a business casual world a few pieces of jewelry, a scarf, a color-coordinated outfit, and an appropriate looking polished shoe, present the image that:

- You know what you are doing.
- You are confident in what you are doing.
- You care enough to make the effort to present yourself professionally.

Accessories can bring a simple pair of khakis and a plain t-shirt one step above to a level that shows that you care what you look like. On the other side, accessories can be overdone and, instead of a classic appearance, you move into the realm of a cartoonish exaggeration of a character from a bad sitcom. Remember to limit your accessories to just a few:

- a watch
- a pair of simple earrings
- a scarf or necklace
- one or two rings
- maybe a bracelet

The Sisterhood of the "Secret Scarf Society"

Have you ever wandered by the scarf selection at a fine department store and wondered to yourself, who wears those things? Can I afford to buy them? Would I look good in one? I found my first scarf at a friend's garage sale. It was a large square scarf suitable for *"shawling"* over a coat or blazer. (*"Shawling"* I'll explain in a moment.) I took it home, hung it over a chair and stared at it for weeks. Finally I gently folded it and put it in a drawer. Another month passed and I could almost hear it calling me every time I opened the drawer. Finally I took out my navy blue blazer, hung it over a chair, and dressed the jacket with the scarf as a shawl. That evening, for a meeting at church, I put on the jacket and shawl. A friend approached and said, "Joyce, I love your scarf. I never know how to wear them but love to see them on people." Thus began my introduction as a sister of the "Secret Scarf Society" *(SSS)*.

Success Secret #8

Start wearing scarfs. There is no real secret to wearing a scarf. Put it on. Decide what feels comfortable to you. Then carry it off with attitude! No fussing or fidgeting allowed!

Occasionally someone will suggest a new way to tie a scarf. Don't take it as a negative on the way you have yours tied. They usually just want to share and to let you know they too are sisters of the *SSS*.

A Suitable Start

Next I acquired a "lapel" scarf. This is the one I usually recommend to beginners. Find a scarf that appeals to you and is in the right color family for your outfits. Lay it under the lapels of your jacket and march out the door with your head held high. Because of my history as a battered woman, the first march out the door was significant. The little negative gremlins in my head kept repeating the negative things I had been told for 20 years. And the negative things I told myself, *"Who do you think you are? You don't know how to wear that thing, everyone will laugh."* BUT no one did laugh. The positive comments stroked my desire for more and I became a scarf addict. I should warn you of that part of the *SSS*. The colors and the way a scarf can tie together the pieces can move the entire outfit one or two steps beyond the ordinary, and can be exhilarating!

I still find scarves at yard sales, estate sales, consignment shops and thrift shops carefully folded and still in the box. I suspect they were purchased on a whim and then laid in the drawer haunting the purchaser until—in a fit of frustration—they were given away. Move them out of the drawers and closets. Put them on, ladies! I have included illustrations of several simple ties. More ideas can be found in scarf-tying tip pamphlets lying in dresser drawers all over America!

Okay, I Have a Scarf. Now What Do I do With It?

Here are several simple ties to begin experimenting with.

Long lapel scarves can

- most easily be laid under the lapel of a jacket or blazer for the beginner.
- tied in front in a simple square knot or overhand knot.
- doubled and pull the ends through the created loop.
- double wrapped around the neck and tied in a simple knot.

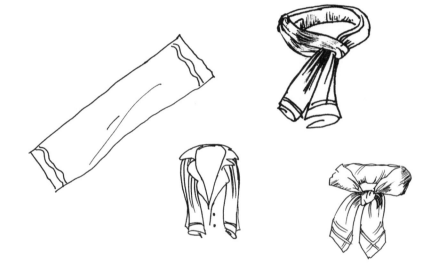

Large square scarves can be

- folded into a triangle and *"shawled"* over a top or jacket, either left to hang down or tied in a knot in front or to the side.

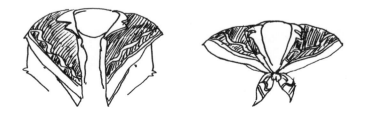

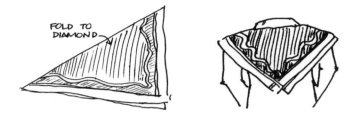

FOLD TO DIAMOND

- folded into a triangle and worn under a jacket as a blouse effect.

- Used to create a long, lapel-like scarf if you fold two sides into the center.

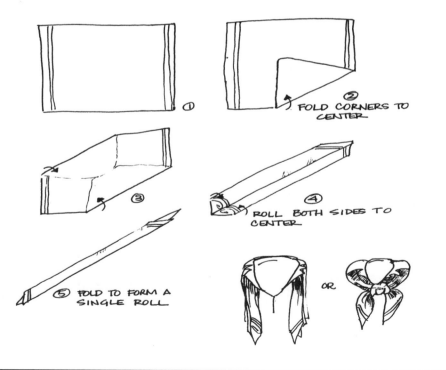

①

② FOLD CORNERS TO CENTER

③

④ ROLL BOTH SIDES TO CENTER

⑤ FOLD TO FORM A SINGLE ROLL

OR

Small square scarves can be:

- folded into the center creating a long ribbon to wrap around your neck, placing the knot in front or off to one side.
- folded into center, knotted in the middle, placing the knot in the middle of your throat and tying the ends in back of your neck, creating a necklace effect.

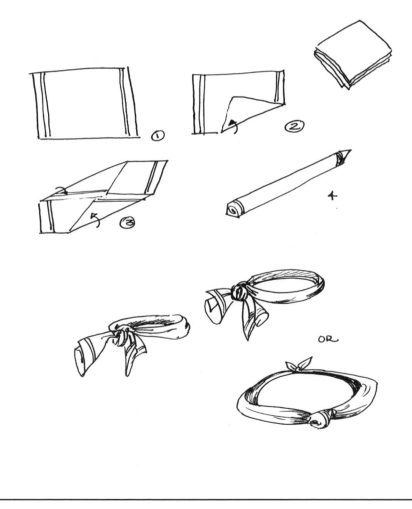

Fabrics

100% silk or soie scarves are generally hand rolled along the edge. Usually the colors are brighter on the top side and can have a variety of different feels—all of them very nice to the touch. Silk scarves will frequently say "dry clean only". I have had success with washing them by hand in cold water with a gentle detergent or dish soap and then ironing them on the 'silk' setting while still damp. I find I very seldom need to wash them, unless they accidentally served as my bib during a meal.

Wool scarves can come in a variety of weights, from a summer weight to a heavy weight suitable for *"shawling"* over a coat in the winter.

Rayon and polyester scarves are made all over the world, come in lovely colors, and can be just as soft and delicate to the touch as silk. They are usually machine stitched along the edge. I do find some polyester scarves will have a slight scratchy feel. Hold it against your cheek to see if the scarf adversely affects you, as scarves are frequently worn close to your face or neck.

If you are concerned that the scarf will slip around on you, hold it in place with a pierced earring hidden in the fold of the fabric. Special little pins can also be purchased for this. I find them frequently at garage sales and thrift shops.

Organizing Scarves

I like to hang the long lapel scarves from a plastic hanger especially designed for this purpose with round holes in it. In the beginning I used a paper-covered hanger and punched holes to pull the scarves through. I keep the hanger on a hook in my bedroom near my mirror. Not only does the rack of scarves look pretty, but they also are close by and not easily overlooked while dressing in the morning. I have also used a regular plastic hanger for hanging scarves and even a standing quilt rack, should you have one.

And, yes, they can be neatly folded and kept in a drawer but I don't think you are as apt to wear them frequently. To avoid creases, you can wrap them around empty paper cylinders you save when finished with your paper towel roll.

Jewelry: Classy or Trashy

Watches

Watches are a recommended piece of jewelry. I have been told by *Ready for Success* volunteers who work in Human Resources departments that wearing a watch shows a sense of time to an interviewer. Of course the first trick is to be sure and show up on time for the interview! Watches come in some very nice gold and silver combinations, allowing you to match both types of jewelry with one. Some women have told me they are allergic to the base metal many watches are made of. This allergy is usually to nickel, so look for a quality watch with a stainless steel back. A leather strap watchband is sometimes a better choice if your skin is sensitive. Applying clear nail polish to the exposed metal helps some people with metal allergies. Or wear the watch bracelet-style as it doesn't sit too tightly against the skin. As it moves more freely this may avoid a reaction from developing.

Earrings

If you wear earrings, only two earrings should be worn to an interview—one in each ear lobe. In other words avoid multiple earrings. Keep the earrings you choose to wear simple. Refrain from wearing those that dangle below the chin line. Earrings should be one inch or less in length. This is an area I advise new employees to watch for a while. Get to know your employer before trying your big dangling earrings and multiple pierced jewelry. If the first comment you get is, "nice earrings," with a slight edge of sarcasm, save those earrings for datewear.

Necklaces

The rule with necklaces is the same—keep it simple. Interesting necklaces are more accepted in the workplace but can be very distracting if they make a lot of noise as you walk or overpower your clothing. If the print on your top is bold, keep the accessories quiet. Bolder necklaces are carried off better against a quieter, solid background.

Bracelets

Bracelets should be limited, in the beginning, to one or two. If your job requires a lot of keyboarding, avoid clanging or rattling bracelets altogether. The noise can be very disturbing to people around you.

Brooches or Pins

Brooches and pins are items of jewelry that can really allow your individual interests to come alive and create conversation starters at a new job. If you choose a really interesting brooch or pin, limit your other jewelry to simple earrings and maybe a necklace. Pins can be found in your grandmother's jewelry box or maybe even in one of your own that you've not looked in for a long time. You can even make them from large, outdated earrings, by popping off the clip or post and gluing on a pin back. Brooches, pins, and even earrings that would make interesting pieces can frequently be found at consignment, garage sales and clearance racks.

Handbags: *Size Does Matter*

Handbags are no longer required to match your belt and shoes. Choosing a handbag in a size that fits your needs in your base wardrobe color is sensible. Some women still change purses daily to match their outfits but more and more women today use just one or two bags, choosing the base color of their shoes as their guide. Changing purses daily is just too time consuming.

I do suggest taking a small handbag to an interview, unless you take a briefcase, and then don't take a handbag at all. A large overflowing handbag at an interview gives the impression of disorganization. Remember it is all about the impression. If you can fit a small notebook, your keys, identification (especially a social security card required for the job application), small amount of money or checkbook, a written list of references with name and numbers, and pen into your purse that should be all you need.

I tend to carry too large a bag for daily use but I frequently will have a smaller bag in my car to put just the essentials in if I want to make a better impression. Unload your purse. Are there things you can do without? This is my biggest mistake. I always seem to think I need everything in there. Even though I wind up fumbling through the collection to find what I am looking for thus creating the image of disorganization.

To Belt or Not to Belt?

Belts should be worn if your pants have belt loops. I suggest avoiding contrasting colors of belts if you and your waist are happier without the emphasis. If you are short-waisted, a belt to match your top will give you the appearance of added length. If you are long-waisted, match the belt to your pants to shorten up the appearance of your torso and lengthen your leg. Wide, low-slung belts with short crop tops exposing the belly button fall into the datewear category. If you don't have a belt to match your pants, tuck in the top, and blouse it slightly over the exposed loops. This is a better choice than the totally wrong belt.

Shoes deserve their very own chapter

... and they shall have one!

Chapter Five

Shoes Are Not Thine Enemy!

❧❧❧❧

Shoes always make a statement when you enter a room. Fortunately today the world recognizes that women with sore feet are not great employees. Tottering into a room on four-inch heels you are unaccustomed to wearing creates the appearance of dressing up from your mother's closet. The other end of the spectrum is arriving in badly worn shoes or tennis shoes (even those in colors). Putting on a pair of running shoes for a walk at lunch, wearing them in from the car, riding the bus or public transit is acceptable, but change to a basic shoe once in the office.

Shoes can be fun fashion statements but keep in mind the basic rule of many work places: no open-toe shoes. The exposure of your toes, even with a lovely pedicure and nail polish, diminishes the authority you might command when you walk into the room. Women might comment on your cute shoes, or even the color of your nail polish. Men tend to see it as a frivolous thing in which women indulge themselves. I would suggest not being seen in the workplace as frivolous. It will not command the respect and positive attention you should be seeking from your employer. There is a current trend to wear a cute strappy little sandal with a business suit in the summer. I suggest you follow this trend in your workplace only if the owner or president of the company does.

Otherwise throw such shoes into a bag and wear them out to dinner. Remember, what is the image you want to project? Are cute strappy little sandals projecting power, authority and professionalism?

Success Secret #9

Wear appropriate shoes. Other women may admire a cute open-toed shoe with a lovely pedicure but many men will view that attention to your feet as frivolous or you're trying to look sexy. Is that how you want to be viewed in your workplace?

Begin building your shoe wardrobe with a quality pump with a two-inch heel or less in basic black. If the shoe is really comfortable for you, a good fit for your foot and budget, buy them in brown and navy. The addition of white stitching, buckles, tassels, and multi-tones on shoes tend to look casual and limit their use in your wardrobe. Those extra shoe selections become ones you add as you find a dependable source for your shoes or at a very reasonable shoe sale. Many fine department stores will have shoe clearance rooms and regular sales in quality shoes.

Remember when buying off the sale rack, the right shoe has probably been tried on several times. If it is real leather it may have stretched and feels very comfortable. My left foot is about a half size larger than my right, so before purchasing shoes, I always need to try on both shoes, expecting the left to be slightly tighter. Leather shoes will stretch with use, so my question when trying on shoes is, will the left become as comfortable as the right? If you have a real distinct difference in your foot size, fit the larger foot and pad the shoe which is smaller with tissue or specially designed heel inserts. I also determine what weight of sock or nylon I will be wearing with the shoe. With my basic shoe for work, I either wear nylons or a trouser sock—never a heavy cotton sock. Wearing heavier socks will stretch out the leather shoe and they will feel too big or sloppy the next time I wear nylons or trouser socks with them. If they are tennis shoes or very casual shoes that I expect to wear with heavy socks, then I keep a pair of those socks tucked in the shoes for that walk at lunch.

I don't care how cute the shoe or how good the deal is, I don't buy them if they are too big or too small. Wearing shoes too big causes you to shuffle when you walk. Shoes that are too small (besides the obvious pain) over time cause problems for the feet that will then limit your shoe choices even more. Remember no shoes are a great deal if they sit in your closet unworn. Even the finest shoe manufacturer can make some ugly, uncomfortable shoes.

Shoes purchased for the workplace:
- should be comfortable to wear for at least eight to ten hours.
- classic in design.
- able to match a multitude of outfits.
- present a professional appearance.

Caring for Your Shoe Investment

Shoetrees are a good addition to your closet wardrobe. Shoetrees are either plastic, metal or wood, are adjustable in size and fit in your shoes to help them hold their shape. I have found fitting shoetrees into a new of pair of shoes allows them to stretch slightly and will improve their wearablity. If the shoes need just a little stretching now is the time to wear them around the house wearing heavy cotton socks. They should feel much better the next time you wear them with trouser socks or nylons. Stuffing them with newspaper very tightly until the next time you wear them will also help stretch out a pair of leather shoes.

Keeping your shoes on racks in your closet allows you to see and quickly select shoes appropriate for your outfit. I have never had enough closet space, but one woman I know keeps each pair of shoes in the original box with a snapshot stapled to the end of the box for easy viewing. Some women use the clear shoeboxes available from discount stores or closet stores, with the same idea of protecting the shoes while allowing for easier selection. I do suggest leaving shoes sit out in the open for about 24 hours after wearing them to allow a reasonable airing out. Shoes will last longer if you can rotate their use frequently.

Success Secret #10
Shoes last longer with regular polishing and rotating their use! Well-tended shoes say a lot about your attention to detail and concern about your appearance.

One of our volunteers, Gretchen, who worked primarily with clothing happened by as a woman and her personal shopper were making a shoe selection. The woman had selected a nice black leather shoe. The clothing specialist, noticing they needed polishing, quickly grabbed the shoes and polished them. The woman smiled as her shoes now looked new. A couple months later she returned for her second visit and upon seeing Gretchen, kicked off her shoes and said, "Can you polish my shoes again?" Gretchen laughed, "I'll be happy to show you how to polish them yourself!"

There are some new products allowing you to polish different colors of shoes with the same clear leather protection. These can be purchased from quality shoe stores or shoe repair shops. They are expensive but my experience, quickly polishing six pairs of shoes and the resulting improvement in appearance, has made the investment worthwhile. The products also tend to last a long time. These products work well on a fine leather purse or leather jacket you may have found at a garage or estate sale but in need of a little attention.

Traditional shoe polish comes in small round jars of crème, small tins of harder wax consistency and bottles. Each of these is a predetermined color to use on a special color of shoe. I suggest brushing off the dirt on the shoe, applying a thin layer of polish with a soft rag, allowing it to dry, wiping it with another clean rag, and finishing with a rapid buffing using a shoe brush or soft clean rag. I have found little differences other than in the application between the three types of colored polishes.

"Synthetic," not leather, shoes can be cleaned using a little window spray cleaner or any other household spray cleaner. Patent leather shoes clean up the best using a small amount of petroleum jelly rubbed into the surface. Suede or fabric shoes clean up best when brushed with a soft brush to remove dirt and stains.

Shoe repair shops are becoming harder and harder to find and usually are expensive. If you tend to wear out your heels quickly or need a slight stitch repair, I would suggest an estimate first. If you find a good quality shoe repair with reasonable prices, let me know. I'm always seeking the quality workmanship that is difficult to find today.

Consider good quality shoes a worthwhile investment. If you live in a part of the country where it rains or snows frequently, consider wearing boots to work and changing once you arrive at the office. Watermarks and salt stains can be removed from leather shoes using a half water/half vinegar solution but such stains rarely come off of fabric shoes. If you have shoetrees put them in wet shoes so they retain their shape while drying, or simply stuff them with newspaper.

Shoes protect our feet. Their appearance says something about your attention to detail and can project a negative image when they are too casual, too fancy, too dirty or too damaged.

Chapter Six

Keeping Up Appearances

Employers and co-workers are willing to forgive and learn to overlook many things about the way you present yourself, as long as your presentation is clean and your work ethic is sterling. BUT I cannot emphasis enough how important it is that when you go in for the interview and EVERY DAY of work, you take the time to prepare yourself. The details create an image of organization, care for your appearance and, thus, for your job and employer. Remember you are representing not only your employer but also yourself.

Success Secret #11

Pay attention to the details of your personal appearance. Whether you work in a very professional setting or a more casual setting, the details are important.

Your Hands

Are your nails trimmed and even? They don't have to be long and perfect. In fact, if you are applying for a position that requires a lot of keyboarding, long nails sometimes give the impression they will interfere with your job performance. (Remember I said "the impression." Grow them back once you have the job and have the opportunity to prove they don't interfere with your job performance.) If you are trying to enter the medical field, I would not recommend artificial nails. The concerns that arose from trapped bacteria several years ago still make some people nervous. Carry a small emery board or nail file to repair those last minute nicks and tears. Filing their nails regularly has helped some women overcome the nail biting habit.

Are your nails clean? If you like to do a lot of gardening, wear garden gloves. Wear gloves when painting or working with harsh cleaning materials or chemicals around the house. Keep a nailbrush near your bathroom sink and use it.

Nail polish? Keep to simple natural colors, although some shades might be accepted such as reds, deep pinks or oranges. Definitely avoid, purple, green, black, and blue. If your nail polish is chipped, remove it all.

Keep in mind you will be shaking hands with many people, especially while interviewing. Use a little light lotion if you have dry hands but not as you walk in the door of the interview. Use it earlier allowing time for it to absorb. Most of us have problems with our palms sweating when we get nervous anyway so you probably don't need a heavy lotion. If you have sweaty palms, carry a tissue or dry washcloth to use prior to going into the interview.

Success Secret # 12
Learn to shake hands–firmly–positively!
It is an important first impression. Many employers
will judge you by your handshake.

We don't teach our daughters to shake hands as we do our sons. I remember early in *Ready for Success's* development, a very good male friend and supporter pulled me aside and said," Joyce, you need to learn how to shake hands." I was expected to meet and greet people representing *Ready for Success* but I would get nervous with every handshake. Was I doing it right? Would they know I didn't know what I was doing? I would look down or away avoiding eye contact. Practice has improved that handshake. Now I shake hands with confidence, including my daughters' friends—to their surprise.

Shaking Hands

- Extend your right hand, grasping the right hand of the recipient of your handshake. Hold your wrist taut. Shake with your lower arm, not your hand.
- The grasp should be firm—not smashing.
- Look them in the eye, SMILE, and relax your grip to release.

It is acceptable to cover your right hand slightly with your left, as a show of warmth or affection.

This is a good time to repeat your name and that of the person you are meeting. It helps to imprint names in your memory with physical touch.

Always wear your name badge on the right shoulder, during the handshake. Your name will be more easily visible and, again, memorable.

Your Hair

Clean hair is very important. Your hair frames your face and adds or detracts quickly to that first impression. Keep your hair clean. If you don't, it will be one of the first things noticed.

If you have long hair, pulling it back will add to the professional appearance. Several years ago there was a commercial advertising shampoo. The woman, you may remembered, untied her hair on the way out of the office to meet her friends at a restaurant. That is datewear vs. daywear, once again.

A good professional hair cut can help solve many hair problems. Search out a salon that teaches hair cutting and styling. Usually the prices are cheaper as the students learn on you. They are watched over by a professional, experienced stylist so it can be worth the "risk". I have used such beauty or cosmetology schools. I once found a young student I liked so much I followed her to her first place of employment and eventually her own business.

If you are into the wildly colored or spiked hair, you might consider one of the rinse-out colors for your weekend fun. Remember, you are representing your employer and what the wild colors say about you, may not be what your employer wants your hair to say about their business.

Your Body

Clean, regular bathing does not mean just once a week or on Saturday night. Avoid heavy perfumed scents. Soap and water daily will do the trick.

Many workplaces have become sensitive to scent-allergies for their employees. Save your special colognes and perfumes for your social life, not the workplace.

The lack of, or failure of, deodorant is a topic that can be sensitive to discuss with even your closest friends. Americans spend huge sums of money to cover, disguise and hide their body odors. You might ask someone close to you if they recommend a particular brand of deodorant as you are considering a brand change. A quick, positive response will tell you to begin seeking stronger odor protection.

Even baking soda patted on under arms can help control body odor. Small packets of baby wipes can be very useful for a quick clean up for personal hygiene. They come in many pleasing scents—and even unscented. Strong offensive body odors can also signal ill health.

Your Face

Another delicate topic is facial hair removal. In this country we find excessive hair on the face very distracting on a woman. There are a number of products available for hair removal. Most of them have to be tested to see what works on your skin type. I will admit that once you begin removing the hair on your chin or upper lip, it will be ongoing. The hair frequently gets coarser and darker as it regrows. Bleaching facial hair is another option that needs to be repeated every few weeks or months.

Easy on the make-up! A little mascara in black or brown,

a little lipstick in a color leaning towards natural (in other words no black, cherry red, bright frosted pink) should be enough. If you wear foundation, keep it very natural looking. Limit strong blush to evening wear.

Your smile matters! If your teeth are in need of repair, you might search out a medical school that teaches dentistry. They frequently offer reduced rates. You become a subject for the student to work on but under the watchful eye of a more experienced and usually able dentist. You might also search out a private dentist who will allow you to pay your bill in monthly installments.

Brush your teeth! Floss, too. And brush your tongue! *(This is one you may not have heard of before.)* Doing this every morning and evening will improve your great smile and breath. Bad breath can be a sign of tooth decay, sinus infection and other health issues. See your doctor if regular dental hygiene does not clear up your breath.

Success Secret #13

SMILE. Your smile is the most important thing you will put on for your interview and job! If you are not comfortable smiling around strangers, practice!

Show me a woman with a smile on her face and eyes reflecting the knowledge that she looks good and I'll show you a beautiful woman!

Your Body Piercings

I recommend just one earring in each ear lobe at interviews. Before wearing multiple ear piercings to work, let them get to know you first. Save the multiples for datewear or social events.

Face piercing jewelry is also best removed for the interview process. Some employers have strict policies concerning facial piercings. Follow the policy of the employer after being hired. Tongue piercings, in particular, can affect your speech. Effective and clear communication is important in the interview as well as on the job.

Other body piercings, such as a belly button piercing, is something your coworkers need never know about. You should never reveal your belly button in the workplace anyway! That goes for other body piercings also.

Your Tattoos

I have worked with many young women who regret the tattoos on their hands, wrists, arms, and ankles because of the past lifestyle they now represent. Some of them prefer to wear long sleeves to cover the arm and wrist tattoos. Others have chosen long skirts or pants to hide the ankle and leg tattoos. Covering the tattoos on hands is the most difficult. Make-up or actual removal is then necessary. If your tattoos represent a lifestyle you now hope to move beyond, see if there is an organization that supports and promotes tattoo removal in your area. While tattoos have become more socially acceptable, even fun light ones send a message in our society due to the possible connection to gangs and violence. Corporate and conservative employers seldom find them acceptable.

Success Secret #14

Never put a tattoo where it can be seen
in an interview.

Your Lingerie

Lingerie is meant to be worn *UNDER* clothing, not as outerwear, despite what fashion magazines may tell you. We met women almost daily at *Ready for Success* in need of undergarments. Proper fitting undergarments are more comfortable and provide support under your clothing to present a more appropriate appearance. Here are a few thoughts on lingerie for a working wardrobe:

• How deeply is your panty cutting into you and where? Are you revealing the type of underwear you have on? Pants or skirts that are too tight will more easily reveal a panty line.

• Bright or dark colored panties worn under light colored pants and skirts will reveal themselves. So will wildly colored prints. Is that the image you want to portray? Are you revealing the type of underwear you have on?

• Brightly colored, dark or wildly patterned bras will show through light colored tops and blouses. These styles become datewear—not daywear.

• If you have a difficult time with the upper thighs rubbing together and causing chaffing, try a panty shaped like a small short. The style is popular now and can even be found in the women's department. Male boxer pants may work for you. Who would know?

• Flesh colored or champagne colored bras are a good choice under white blouses. This will depend on your skin tone.

• Padded bras are sometimes referred to as "modesty bras." The padding also helps disguise the protruding nipple.

• Wear the right size bra. The industry estimates 70% of women are wearing the wrong size bra. Bra manufacturers regularly send representatives out to fine department stores to measure women for the proper fit. These events are usually free to the public. Of course they are hoping to convince you to buy a bra but this information can be extremely helpful the next time you are searching the discount racks.

A Proper Fitting Bra

Measure under your breasts around your rib cage, and add 2 inches. This should give you the number dimension (32, 34, 36, 38, 40, 42, etc.) for your bra size. If you are between those numbers move up to the next size. Then measure around the fullest part of your breast. If the measurement is one inch more you are an A cup; 2 inches—a B cup; 3 inches—a C Cup; etc. The biggest mistake I saw women making at *Ready for Success* is wearing a bra that is too small or not pulling their straps up firmly to provide the anti-gravity support most of us need. Bras do come in sizes 48DD to 54 F—they are just harder to find and more expensive. Extended sizes are best purchased through catalogs, online or in specialty shops. Your bra should hook on the middle row of hooks. Bra extenders can be purchased in most fabric stores. They simply add another 1-2 inches by hooking onto the hook system.

- Don't forget your bra size will go up and down as your weight changes.

- Camisoles are a great addition to a lingerie wardrobe. They can add cover to a colored bra, provide warmth under a light blouse, prevent a scratchy sweater from annoying you, and provide a more modest look under a thin blouse.

Care Tips

Wash bras and camisoles in the gentle cycle in the washing machine or by hand. Line dry them to last longer. Most bras contain spandex, which is slowly destroyed by the heat of a dryer. I always hook the hooks and place my bras in a mesh bag when washing them in the machine. Use the hooks you don't normally use when wearing the bra. They will stay hooked better during the wash cycle. Without the lingerie bag, the hooks can become entangled with other articles of clothing, ruining them. Adding 1/2 cup white vinegar to the wash will help remove perspiration stains too. I have a towel rack hanging above my washer to place my bras on as they come out of the gentle cycle.

Panty Hose, Nylons and Tights

I suggest dark pairs in the winter that match your shoes and skirts, creating a long line. I like lighter ones matching my skirt or natural colors in the summer with lighter shoes. If I am wearing a black skirt in the summer, I will chose off-black panty hose or a natural color with black shoes.

Many women select one size larger in panty hose for extra comfort. Buying multiple pairs of panty hose in the same color can save you money, if one leg runs, save it until one leg runs in another matching pair. Then clip off the legs with runs about thigh high, slip on one pair and then the other. You'll be wearing double panty tops (better tummy control), but each leg will be covered without a run.

Buy trouser socks on sale. Trouser socks are thin nylon-like knee-hi's that work wonderfully under slacks and long skirts. They give a nice line to your ankle, are not too heavy in your shoe, and create a more polished look than bare legs or natural colored nylons. They come in extended sizes for women with heavier legs or larger feet.

Caring for Your Clothing

Remember, this is your work uniform. Take care of it and it will last longer and serve you well. When buying from clearance racks, thrift stores, or wherever, you will have a considerable investment not only in dollars but in working towards a better future.

- Change clothes as soon as you come home. Now is the time to wear your jeans and t-shirts with those cute logos.
- Hang up anything that is wearable for another day: the blazer, possibly the pants, and certainly anything that is "dry clean only". Don't move them directly to the closet. Hang them from the shower pole, or on a hook outside your closet to allow them to air out for 24 hours.
- Place tops, trouser socks etc., directly in the laundry pile, noting any spots in need of pre-treatment. Painter's tape works well to mark a spot for spot removal before washing. Just don't leave it on for over a week.
- Slip into your fun shoes and let your work shoes air out.
- If the bottoms of your pants are becoming exceptionally frayed and dirty, you are wearing them too long!

Dry Cleaning

There are some very good products out there for "dry clean only" clothing to use in your home dryer. I have found them most useful for odor removal and freshening.

- Check to see if there are self-serve dry cleaners in your area.

- Look for dry cleaning coupons and advertised specials.

Spots on "dry clean only" are still best removed by the dry cleaner. When you take in dry cleaning, be sure to point out the spot and, if possible, name the culprit. I had a lovely silk blouse I spilled oil and vinegar on; I took it to the dry cleaner, pointed out the spot and mentioned what I had spilled on it. I was delighted to get it back with no evidence of my need for a bib. Hiding the spots so the dry cleaner doesn't know what a messy eater you are doesn't help them remove the spots.

Don't have your clothing dry cleaned more than necessary, certainly not after each use, unless you have a stain. Dry cleaning chemicals are hard on the fabric, and you. Always remove the dry cleaning bag and dispose of it. Allow the clothing to air out before you wear it.

I have successfully hand washed or used the gentle cycle on my washing machine for silk blouses and sweaters. I even throw them in the dryer on no-heat to fluff out wrinkles and then hang or lay flat to finish drying. Special delicate washing solutions are available from some finer department stores for washing silk. They are expensive but considering the cost of replacing a silk blouse, may be worth the investment.

Warning: Frequent washing or dry cleaning of just one piece in a suit combo will probably fade or slightly discolor that piece. BUT if you are wearing it frequently you are probably getting your money out of the piece. Just be aware of the possibility of fading and discoloration.

I once overheard a woman at *Ready For Success* commenting that she did not want a linen suit because she couldn't afford to have it dry cleaned. Her personal shopper commented, "None of us can. Besides, they wrinkle again so quickly. The thing with a linen suit is that they give the appearance that you can afford to have them dry cleaned, so wearing them slightly wrinkled is acceptable."

Little Things that Count

- Smoking odors can be terribly offensive to non-smokers. If you smoke, quit! Use the money you save to improve the quality of your wardrobe.
- Put used dryer sheets in a small plastic bag and carry them in your purse or car for a quick rub against your trouser socks or panty hose to prevent static cling. Commercially available spray products are effective also.
- Pet hair can be difficult to remove and it leaves the impression that you are careless about your presentation. With two dogs and two birds, I am always struggling with pet "give-aways" on my clothing. I carry a roller with tape wrapped around it to remove the hair before I leave my vehicle. These rollers are available from most discount stores. The sheets tear off as they become covered with hair and lint. Masking tape wrapped around your hand sticky-side-up also works very well.
- Don't stick name tags on leather or suede clothing. It will leave a mark and sticky residue when removed.
- Be sure to remove sticky name tags from your clothing before washing, the washing removes the paper backing but leaves a sticky residue which is very difficult to remove.

- Need an emergency hem? Scotch tape works well for a temporary fix on most fabrics. If you are not handy with a needle and thread, fusible tape is available in the sewing department. Lay the tape along the edge of the fabric, fold over and iron. The tape melts into place holding the hem— even through washings.
- Try a lint brush on heavier fabric soiled with dried-on mud or food. It can sometimes be brushed off.
- The size of shoulder pads can really date a blazer or jacket. Removing shoulder pads from jackets and blazers is a risk. Usually the construction and cut of the jacket are dependent on the body the shoulder pads give the garment. Occasionally you can replace the larger shoulder pads in jackets with smaller ones. Make certain it doesn't leave extra fabric wrinkled at the top of the garment.

Laundering Tips

- Learn to use an iron.
- Try one of the new wrinkle release products. Some find it especially helpful on khakis.
- Remember to remove clothing promptly from the dryer before it cools off, and the wrinkles are set. Over-drying clothing will set wrinkles in some polyester fabrics. If you have forgotten to remove the clothing in a timely manner, a quick fluff on "no heat" may help. Or throw in a damp towel and re-dry. Shake the clothing after removing from the dryer before putting on a hanger. This will also help to remove wrinkles.

- If your water is rusty, add one of the rust remover products to the wash water, especially with your lighter colors.
- If you use public washers and dryers, search the insides for nasty surprises left behind before you put in your clothing.
- Empty all pockets before washing clothing. An uncapped marker from a child's pocket has damaged a couple of my nice tops.
- Blazers and jackets are difficult to iron. Hang them in the bathroom while showering and the steam will usually help remove the wrinkles.
- Remove the shoulder pads from most blouses and tops before washing them. They will stay flat and create a smoother look longer. Use Velcro to reattach them.

I have found the new bleach pen product extremely helpful in removing small stains from white tops.

Button, Button, Who's Got the Button?

Buttons are a dead giveaway. Pay attention to them. Often they are not sewn on well. Reinforce them BEFORE the threads break and you loose the button. For those that get heavy duty use—like on coats—consider using dental floss as thread for reinforcement.

- When wearing a double breasted jacket, button the inside button first and the jacket will hang straighter. Think of David Letterman and his habit of unbuttoning and buttoning his inside button on his double-breasted jacket during his monologue.

- Lose a button to a special piece? If possible, move the bottom button to the top. This is usually less noticeable when using a slightly different button on the bottom. Or make the top button something totally different—and eye-catching. It will appear to be intentional.
- Replacing poor quality or dressy buttons with more subdued ones will change the look of a blazer or jacket from really dressy to more office casual.
- Many articles of new clothing come with extra buttons attached. If they are sewn inside the piece of clothing, leave them until you need them. If they come in the little packet attached to the tag, tear them off and collect all of them in a glass jar with a lid. You might have to search through several to find the right one, but at least they are all in one place. Or write a description of the clothing item on the packet.

I once purchased a beautiful size 6 dress for $1.00 at a garage sale. It was obviously not my size but the buttons were a perfect fit for the blazer I had also bought that had ugly buttons. Buttons can be very expensive to purchase new. Think about checking the secondary clothing market for just buttons.

Saving buttons from damaged clothing is a thrifty idea our grandmothers used. Remember all those button jars. Not a bad idea, even today!

Chapter Seven

For the Rubenesque Woman

Rubens was a Flemish Baroque painter in the 17th century whose softly rounded women delight the art world. This period in history glorified the well-endowed woman, with her curves and soft mounds of flesh. After all, it signified that she could afford to eat! So whether we are discussing Ruben*esque*, curvaceous, plus size, or big beautiful women, let's celebrate the gifts all of us have. Be a confident, capable and successful woman and dress that way! Thank you, Oprah!

Success Secret #15

I have yet to meet a woman who thinks she has the perfect body, whether she is size 6, 12, 16, or 24. We waste too much time and energy obsessing about our bodies! Remember the ads with supermodels are even retouched! Let's move on ladies!

First let's clear up some terms and misconceptions in this area: 16 W does not mean 16 WIDE. It means 16 Womens. In the clothing industry 'W' means wide in reference to shoes only. Plus sizes refer to womens sizes usually 16 and above. It is a silly term the fashion industry uses to separate them and us! Not all size 16 or 18 clothing is created equally. A size 16 Junior is not the same as 16 Misses, nor is 16 Womens even close to that same fit. Women of all sizes can vary dramatically in sizes depending on the clothing manufacturer. Yet, it is amazing how many women I work with have a difficult time trying on a garment labeled 18, especially if they are convinced they wear 16. A 16W will generally be more generous in the hips and thighs or bust, if a top. If you happen to be narrower in the hips a 16 Misses may fit better than a 14 Womens. It is time for an industry wide standard of sizing in women's clothing. I have a few ideas, if they would only ask me!

Women of all sizes will frequently have trouble with suits paired in one size. Many women will vary a size or even several sizes between their tops and bottoms. There is nothing wrong with you. It is the manufacturers and clothing stores who insist on selling matching tops and bottoms in sets rather than as separates.

Ruben*esque* women have a reputation for being sloppy. Many of us wear our clothing too loose. Are we trying to hide something? Well, it ain't happening. We only look sloppy. And about that untucked blouse trying to hide our stomachs? We aren't fooling anyone! Tuck it in, blouse it slightly over the waistband, and look in the mirror. Doesn't that look more professional?

At the other end of the fashion spectrum is the woman, usually a young woman more confident in her body, who is trying to wear the latest thing from "teen haven"—only in a size too small so that excess flesh rolls over the waistband and out from under the top. This does not create an appropriate appearance for the work environment. Remember, there *IS* a difference between datewear and daywear! Of course, even size 6 should not be showing the flesh between one's top and bottom at work.

Ruben*esque* women can look confident and professional just as their slimmer counterparts. I will admit it can be more of a challenge and takes more work. The clothing industry is catching on that these beautiful women are seeking decent clothing. Unfortunately, just as very petite women—those who wear size 2 —have trouble finding suitable clothing in mature styles, very large women are sometimes forced to choose fabrics and styles that are less than complimentary and professional in appearance.

Many upscale clothing manufacturers are designing and manufacturing improved options for the big, beautiful working woman. Those items are still very difficult to find in thrift stores, garage sales, and consignment stores. When I began my search for a navy blue blazer in 1996, I searched the secondary clothing market extensively for size 22. I found a few, but many were worn out or damaged beyond my ability to repair. It took me nearly 6 months of searching to find what I was looking for and, believe me, in those days I did not have the clothing experience I have now, nor my current standards for a good fit and quality clothing. Finding quality blazers in the moderately priced retail market is still a big challenge.

Dressing Tips

- Choose a solid color for your top and bottom; then layer a blazer or beautiful tailored open blouse over the top.

- Don't be afraid to try a short bolero jacket with pants or a skirt. I have had women swear they would expose too much of their "caboose" with such an outfit, yet when the blazer and bottom match in a solid color, the result can be very attractive.

- Tuck in the blouse! I have heard all the excuses not to but

I have seen the positive results even more. Just remember to blouse it slightly. Tucking it tightly only accentuates the uncomfortable look and feel. And stand up straight! Slouching only rolls the tummy out more and emphasizes the negative area.

- If you are one of the lucky ones with great legs, don't be afraid to show them with knee length skirts—just not too short or too tight. You want to be able to sit down in them discreetly. Just below the knee is a great length.

- Draw attention to your face with a scarf, lovely pin or earrings.

- If you are a plus petite, learn how to hem or exchange services with someone who does. Maybe you could paint their kitchen! Keep your shoes, socks and pants one color to add the illusion of height. If your waistband will be hidden, roll it to bring the crotch of the pants or hem of the skirt up to where it belongs.

- Find a good seamstress to work with. That way you can also shop with alteration possibilities in mind.

- Write down the names and labels that work for you. You may wish to search for this name again, even online.

The retail choices are improving for Ruben*esque* women. There is power in our numbers and our dollars. As more women seek out suitable clothing options, demand better choices and refuse to buy the unflattering merchandise offered in some women's departments, the buyers and designers will realize we like the same classic look as size 8—with just a bit more material.

Chapter Eight

Organizing Your Closet to Save You Time and Money

ફ્જફ્જ

I must admit a few years ago I couldn't see the importance of organizing my closet. After all, I only owned a couple dresses and skirts. At *Ready for Success* we had some wonderful volunteers who not only taught me a lot about dressing, but also the importance of organization. You may not have 100,000 pieces of clothing pass through your closet in a year as we did but knowing 1) what you have, 2) what needs to be replaced, and 3) where it is, can be real time and money savers.

Step One: *Completely Empty Your Closet!*

- Does it need additional light? A higher wattage bulb can help. A fresh coat of light colored paint can really brighten a dim interior.
- Are the closet poles within your reach?
- Do you have shelves? Are they within your reach?
- Do you need space for shoes?
- Would a step stool help you reach the top shelves?

Closet organizers can be purchased at many home remodeling businesses and discount stores which will enhance your space and its use.

Step Two: *Seasonal Savvy*

Do you live in an area of the country where there are drastic differences between seasons? Do you have room in your closet for summer and winter season wardrobes? I don't so I acquired a sturdy portable rack I placed in a dry storage area for my off-season clothing. I moved an old dresser near by and placed winter sweaters with sachet bags scattered about the drawers. I placed pieces of cedar from a friend's remodeled cedar closet near the rack to prevent moth and insect infestation. I used a flat storage box on small wheels under the bed for off-season shoes.

Decide which things in your wardrobe are definitely winter or summer. Transitional pieces are sometimes a little harder to make decisions about. Move the off-season things to your designated storage space.

For these long term storage things

- Hang items on plastic hangers. Wire ones will sometimes leave rust marks over the long term.
- Remove all dry cleaner bags. Trapping those chemicals in your clothes is not a good idea.
- Cover the clothing with a clean sheet or old tablecloth to protect them from dust.
- Be sure the area is dry and free of mold.

Step Three: *Return the Clothes to the Closet*

- Check each piece for necessary repairs as you move it back for the current season. Mark the repairs with a safety pin or note, and separate into a repair pile.
- Check items for spots. Identify the spot (dry cleaners frequently use a bright colored painter's tape to prevent damage to the item). If it is washable, try a spot remover or pour white vinegar over it. Rewash and recheck before drying. Drying only sets most spots.
- Are the sweaters or t-shirts pilling or looking worn? These are things you can replace from end-of-season clearance racks.

Step Four: *Be Brutal!*

- How long since you've worn this piece? You might have found a great deal on the sale rack but never really liked the color. Pass it along to someone who will. Maybe it is your size, but is an uncomfortable fit, or the fabric is scratchy. Whatever it is that prevents you from wearing it, get rid of it. Make more room in your closet!
- Does it still fit? Many women I know have their "fat" clothes and their "thin" clothes. If it has been over a year since you have worn one or the other, get rid of them! You probably won't want those particular clothes if you gain or lose more weight anyway!
- If it is out of date, is there anything that could be done to update it? If not, get rid of it. I know women who hang on

to clothing because they think the style will return. That is true, but probably with some new twist, different fabrics, colors, less or more shoulder pads, etc. Pass it along now while there is still some chance for someone else to get some wear out of it.

We attach great sentimental emotion to our clothing; the great deal we found, the outfit we bought with our sister on vacation, the outfit we were wearing when we got the promotion. The list goes on. We see women bringing in clothing all the time at *Ready for Success* that obviously had strong emotional meaning to the donor. That is one of the reasons we sort clothes out of the eyesight of the donor. We fail to see the faults in our own clothing, especially those favorite pieces. So for this step you must be brutal. Once you have sorted your own clothing move on to Step Five.

Step Five: *Sorting by Category*

Return your clothing to your clean, bright closet by hanging them together in sections: all your skirts, all your pants, all your blouses and all your blazers together. Then, within each clothing type, divide your clothing into colors. I always separate the blacks and navy blues by a lighter color like khaki. I have learned by humbling experience that in the morning, black and navy can look the same. I discovered after leaving the house that I was wearing a navy blue blouse with black pants and that was not my intention!

Success Secret #16
Hang the pieces to your suits separately.
You will see them as separates with more choices of
clothing partners within your closet.

I organize my shoes by season and color—checking shoes for those needing repairs, polishing, and replacement. I use the top shelf in my closet for those things I only occasionally need, like a cardigan for a cool summer night. Those are things I don't want to have to move to my off-season storage place since I wear them much less frequently during this season. I usually keep my recreational wear (shorts, jeans, capris, and logo t-shirts) separate from my work wear. These can be folded and placed in dresser drawers.

Hangers

Did you realize hangers are not all created equal? Long-term clothing storage on wire hangers can create a strong, narrow crease in most clothing. And if exposed to moisture can leave unsightly rust marks on your clothing. Wire hangers frequently arrive in your home from the dry cleaner. If you prefer not to use them in your closet, ask if the dry cleaner will take them back to recycle or reuse.

I prefer plastic tubular hangers although they do take up more closet space. Plastic tube hangers can be purchased inexpensively at most discount and dollar stores. The best type of hanger is the thin plastic style found in most retail clothing stores. Ask if you can have the hanger when you purchase your clothing. Many stores will add it to your bag or keep the clothing on it, putting the clothing in a garment bag. This also helps the clothing stay wrinkle-free on the trip home from the store.

Hanging Tips

Many items with large neck openings will slip off hangers.

- Use wire hangers with foam covering.
- Use plastic retail hangers with no-slip pads at the ends.

- Slip the top into the hanger slots provided on some plastic and tube hangers.
- Use wooden clip clothes pins to hold the clothing in place.
- Use safety pins or straight pins to hold the clothing on the hanger.

When hanging pants and skirts, a crease can form by folding them over a wire hanger, let alone the rusty wire mark already mentioned. Try folding them over a cardboard-covered hanger or over a plastic tubular hanger. The broader support leaves fewer marks. I prefer using plastic hangers with clips for my pants and skirts that allow me to hang the pants. Plastic clips can be purchased from the discount stores to go on tube hangers to convert them to pant or skirt hangers. Again, wooden clothes pins or safety pins work also. Wooden and plastic hangers made specifically for pants and skirts can also be found in discount stores. They have a clasp set up to hold the pant between two bars. I hang all my pants folded at the waist to match the front crease of the pants. I like to hang my pants from the waist. Others prefer matching the seams and hanging the pants upside down from the hem. If I am short on hangers for pants and skirts, my better wear goes on the nicer hangers. I fold the jeans and the like for a shelf or drawer. If your waistline is considerably bigger than the hanger, fold the edges around to meet the clips. Hanging a skirt with a lot of extra fabric hanging off the sides allows many fabrics to stretch and affect your hemline.

I use short plastic covers over clothing that tend to collect dust on the shoulders. A lint brush can quickly remove the dust on most clothing, except beaded tops, some wools and silks.

If you happen to have a window in your closet, beware of leaving silk exposed to sunlight. Sunlight fades and discolors the fabric quickly.

Organization is its Own Reward

By having an organized closet I have a clearer picture of what it is I have to wear. By looking in the closet I can see where the gaps might be. Everything in my closet must have at least three buddies to justify its closet space. I actually save money with an organized closet. I can see that I now need to replace a white silk tank top I spilled a little spaghetti sauce on (and even with spot removal is not coming out) so I am keeping my eyes open at sales for such a top. I encourage sale shopping but not for the sake of collecting more clothing. Sale shopping will assist you in building a work wardrobe at reduced costs while upgrading the quality.

Chapter Nine

O.K. I Get the Idea But I Still Can't Afford It!

❧❧❧

In my search for a new way to present myself, I faced the hardest question of all. How can I afford better clothing when I can't afford food or clothing for my children? I certainly could not justify full-price even at discount stores. I began searching out great clothing deals and allowing a small amount as my clothing budget. I discovered that the better I was at bargain shopping, the better I was able to dress my children using those same skills. Of course, the more employable I saw myself, the more the financial rewards would be, the more my children would benefit. So where did I begin?

Fine Department Stores

Are you surprised to see that first on my list? I was too, as a novice-clothing shopper! I will admit that the fine department stores take a little bit more time but the rewards can be awesome! I once felt too intimidated to even walk around a store I knew I could not afford to shop in. I frequently find high quality panty hose for a dollar on the clearance racks of these department stores. Don't be afraid to ask the clerk if they have any clearance or where their clearance racks are. I find great bargains at the end of season sales on name brands in all sizes—even in my large size.

- Scout out department stores that attract you. Spend an afternoon just wandering about the store and familiarizing yourself with the layout. They will usually have high-end merchandise as well as moderately priced merchandise departments. Familiarize yourself with the brand names in each area. Where do they place that clearance merchandise?

- Smile and look directly at the sales associates when they speak to you. Developing a relationship with sales associates can make your shopping experience much easier, pleasant, and rewarding. I have also discovered that many of these stores retain their associates longer so you can work with the same person on future visits. Remember they are working just as hard as you are to earn a living. If you are just thinking about trying on clothes, try not to be too demanding. Hang your clothes back up and place them in the dressing area. The staff frequently prefers to return them to the proper racks to save on confusion. If they are busy, relax and enjoy the visit. Look around until they can get to you. Believe me, they will appreciate your patience. If you have a particularly good person, ask for her card for future visits or to call and ask her directly about a particular piece of merchandise. Do they have a mailing list you can get your name on?

Sales associates will usually share with you:
- what they may know about upcoming sales
- when they put their sale items out

I have had women tell me they felt associates in some of the high-end stores did not always treat them respectfully. I don't go to my favorite department store if I just finished gardening. In other words be clean and presentable. Jeans are perfectly acceptable today but wear clean ones with no rips and decent shoes. One associate I work with frequently told me she can tell by a customer's shoes how serious they are about shopping in that department. Are they presentable? I have to be honest. I did not realize in the beginning of my own search for a professional appearance, just how much my shoes gave me away.

Remember department stores are your research. What is the current blazer form, lapel shape, fabric, color, and color combination? Remember there is a difference between style and fashion. Adding a little color statement in the current fashion color can be fun and will update your wardrobe. I found a bright lime green t-shirt on sale for very little money that I wore under my navy blazer. Adding the "new color" to an old dependable piece updated the whole look. Keep in mind the name brands, fabrics and types of construction you found in the finer department stores. The more educated and informed you are, the more confidence you will have to search for the next level of quality business clothing at the consignment shop.

Success Secret #17

Don't buy it, no matter how great the deal is, if:

- it is the wrong size today even if you are on a diet.
- the color isn't good on you.
- it's the right size but poor fit for your body type.
- it needs alterations, unless the store offers them for free, or you do that type of thing regularly. Don't just add it to your pile to do someday.
- it is still more than your budget allows, unless you will wear it enough times to justify the cost.

The Consignment Shop

These stores usually take gently used clothing from customers and resell it, returning a percentage of the sale to the person who brought in the merchandise. Many are located in upscale areas but not all. *(In Minnesota, a series of stores called "Turnstyles" can be found in many moderate-income areas throughout the metro area.)* Consignment shops are usually very select about what they take in.

- Clothes must be in the best possible shape—nearly new.
- They can actually be new, something never even worn.
- They must be recent or current styles and trends.(An exception here maybe in retro and antique clothing.)

If you're bringing items in, call ahead to find out what season they are taking clothing for, and how it should be brought in (always clean and usually on hangers). These stores usually send out checks for merchandise that was purchased on a monthly or quarterly basis, and usually allow the credit to be applied towards shopping in the store. Some consignment stores take other merchandise besides clothing including jewelry, handbags, even household appliances or knick-knacks. To be honest, I still have found better deals on clearance racks at fine department stores but at consignment stores I do find better quality and prices than at the usual discount store. Ask to be on their mailing list, if they have one. Remember these stores have new things coming in on a daily basis. Many consignment stores lower the prices on items that have been there longer than 30–60 days.

Find a consignment shop with prices and quality you like and in an area that is fairly easy for you to get to. Then stop by on a regular or semi-regular basis. Don't expect to find something every time you go, however, on occasion, someone with your similar taste and size will have brought in clothing that could fill your shopping bag and budget easily.

The associates in many of these stores are owners, part owners, or long time employees. Take the time to get to know them. Let them know the kinds of things you are seeking. I have found some lovely formal wear in these stores for special occasions that have obviously been worn only once.

Moderately Priced Stores and Specialty Shops

These stores will frequently advertise wonderful clearance offers. Most of them are great deals on good products but pay attention to the details of the offer.

Success Secret #18
Sometimes a sale or bargain is not one!
Do the math of a sale

I have frequently found sale signs advertising clothing for 30%-50% off, yet when I examine the price and really look at the clothing, I recognize it as not that great of a deal. In calculating the sale price:

- Does the percentage off apply to the original price of the article or current markdown price?
- Is the sale price already marked or will it be taken at the register?
- To estimate the price at the clearance rack, figure what 10% would be. If the price is $19.99 and the article is 30% off, 10% of 19.99 is almost $2, times 3, thus it would be about $6 off or total price just over $14.00.
- 50%? Divide the price in half. 75%? Divide in half again.
- 80% off? I reverse the earlier suggestion. What is 10% off the price? Almost $2, times 2 equals $4.00 total price.
- Watch the register as your purchase is rung up. Was the price what you expected? If not, why not? It is easier to handle differences at the register rather than coming back later.

I have spent thousands of dollars for the *Ready for Success* program on discounted items and the errors have been numerous! It is worth my time and yours to be sure computer scanners are working properly, clothing is on the right rack, and sale signs are accurate. Politely question differences.

Men's Stores or Departments

Consider shopping men's stores or departments. Usually the tailoring is free. Buttons are traditionally on the other side from women's clothing but, honestly, who will notice? And men's shirts are usually cheaper to dry clean. Men's sizes are more exact and for the plus size women, easier to find larger sizes. Pants in the men's department are not always a good choice for women if the crotch area is cut differently.

Discount Stores

These stores usually contain very good collections of recreational and informal wear at low prices. This is a good place to pick up a plain, no-pocket t-shirt in a fun color, or a basic white or black one to wear under a cardigan, blazer, or vest. The basic khaki and Docker pant can be found here very reasonably, especially if you don't have the time to search for your size and price range from a sale rack. Some stores carry blazers and even suits but usually the better buys are in the more informal wear areas and in lingerie items such as bras and underwear.

Outlet Stores

These stores are normally associated with name brand stores and merchandise. They may carry catalog returns as well as last-season's items that didn't do as well as the store buyers expected. Great deals can usually be found here. Remember that I have still found better deals in the clearance departments of finer department stores. One lingerie manufacturer has an outlet near me offering bras at discounted prices yet I found the same bra on a clearance rack at my favorite department store at half the price being offered by the outlet store. Of course, the price at the outlet mall was 30% off the full price. With practice you will learn which of your favorite products may be found with some regularity for a reasonable price at outlets. I am not a big enough fan of outlet malls to drive a great distance and shop all day. However I will stop if passing by one.

Estate Sales

Estate sales or moving sales are usually better for other types of shopping rather than clothing. The professionals who handle upscale sales tell me antique clothing and some upscale clothing will sell. They themselves are frequently searching for someplace to send their left-overs or even the pre-sale clothing to. These sales usually involve one woman or a family therefore you would have to be lucky to find your size and style preference. BUT, it does happen. If the family themselves are handling the estate sale, they may be willing to negotiate on prices, but rarely if they are using a dealer. You might try leaving your name and number if things don't sell and you think the clothing would be a real asset to your closet. Be forewarned. My experience is the family or dealer wants you take it all at the end of sale, not just pick through for a few pieces. Still these are great places to find silk scarves, costume jewelry, nice handbags and briefcases.

Thrift Stores

These stores normally sell items to support some type of non-profit, church or mission. People donate items and in return they receive a tax write-off. Not everyone is interested in the tax write-off. Many are only seeking a worthwhile agency to support with their clothing or other donations. Frequently the employees here are supplemented by, or are totally, volunteers. They may also be working in some type of retail training program.

The prices might compare with garage sale prices except:
- Usually the weather is less of a factor.
- They have regular hours.
- They have dressing rooms.
- The resources are larger and more varied, thus the choices are better.

Thrift shops can vary widely in quality, quantity, and cleanliness of items. The merchandise changes on an almost daily basis. I encourage you to seek out one near you that meets your standards of organization and cleanliness, and then stop by frequently. Normally these types of businesses do not negotiate on price. They will have great clearance prices and specials, depending on the size of their inventory.

These stores are often seeking help. Depending on the store policy for volunteer purchases, this can be a great opportunity with the additional perk of allowing you regular shopping of their merchandise. (Then don't forget to list volunteering on your resume.)

Garage Sales, Yard Sales, and Church Rummage Sales

I have a long history of garage *sailing* and have logged thousands of miles searching garage sales. Most of my home is furnished in "garage sale chic." Clothing is a more difficult area in which to score big at garage sales. Once again you are dealing with only one woman or a small group of women, so ask when you walk up the drive, if they have the sizes you are searching for.

Garage Sale Shopping Tips

- Measure the shoulder width, sleeve length, pant length, inseam length, rise length and waist of a favorite blouse and pair of slacks. Write down the numbers and carry them in your purse.
- Carry a tape measure to check clothing without trying it on. You can compare the numbers from your list of your favorite pieces, although trying it on is still the best choice. This trick works well for other members of your family too, who may not be into garage *sailing.*
- Ask if you can carry the article of clothing out into the sunlight to check for stains. Most of these types of sales are held in dark garages or poorly lit areas.
- Remember it is very rare to be able to return something for a refund to a garage sale. So if it doesn't work, how much will you be losing when you donate it to a thrift store, sell it at your own garage sale or sell it on eBay.

It Never Hurts to Ask

My standard rule of thumb is to always ask if they will take less. Then suggest a price. Even if they say NO, you can walk away knowing you got the best possible deal on the article. Or go on down the road, and possibly find something cheaper. The last day of the sale, as with an estate sale, is the very best time to negotiate but the poorest selection day. Leave your name and number in case they reconsider, and the price and item are important enough to you. If you are purchasing several things from the same sale ask for a discounted price on all of the things as a group.

Church rummage sales are the exception because multiple families are usually involved. They sometimes also have different areas for different types of clothing. Several annual sales I am very familiar with have special areas for the upscale items and designer names.

Shopping from Your Home or Computer

Catalog shopping is still available to those of you who hate crowds or waiting in line, or whose hours don't work well with traditional store shopping hours. Some of these businesses will accept pre-payment by check or money order, and fewer still will bill you next month for your order. Most require a credit card at the time you order over the phone, or when you mail in your order.

More and more of these companies have gone to "online" sales. Computer shopping, eBay, Internet and catalogue ordering online requires the access to a computer and "the web." If you don't have access to a computer and web/Internet connection, try your local library. Check their policies for usage and online ordering. Many public schools and community education departments offer classes in general computer use to the public. Check if such resources are available to you in your area.

We have used eBay to purchase some lot sizes of new panties and bras for *Ready for Success*. I am not convinced online shopping will replace my wardrobe shopping in actual stores. I still like to see the product, feel the texture, try on the article and compare one real article next to another.

Here are some online shopping tips for you beginners:

- Use a search engine (Google, Yahoo, MSN) to find an eBay list or item, or a particular clothing company or brand.
- Choose a site and browse their offerings. eBay has very clear tips and instructions on their site for using their services. Find out what the abbreviations mean to save you time and effort.
- The more specific you are in your search, the less overwhelming the choices become. Try several different descriptions of articles, including size and color.
- Remember there will be a shipping and handling (and sometimes sales tax, too) cost added to your cost of these items. With this additional charge, it may not be the great deal it appeared to be at first.

I have found one benefit of leaving my name and email address with some of my favorite stores. I receive online coupons that I can print and then use in the store.

How to Pay for It?

Like anything, it is easy to get caught up in the excitement of finding a great clothing deal. I admit that when I began my search for an improved wardrobe, I could not afford groceries. I had two teenage daughters also in need of clothing and wanting the latest fashion trend like their friends. Figuring out how to afford clothing for myself was a real challenge. I was struggling to maintain and find a financial balance with a budget with very little room for error or mistakes! I had declared bankruptcy with the divorce, had no credit cards, and a very poor credit history. I began a serious effort to slowly work my way out of that hole I was in. I limited my clothing purchases to a few dollars a month. I let friends and family know I was seeking clothing in my size. I had to honestly admit what my size was. Shortly after we began *Ready for Success*, two very dear friends blessed me with a shopping trip at their expense. They took me to stores, bought me clothing, bras, panties, camisoles, shoes and even a coat! It was an amazing experience for me personally. I am not sure if those two friends ever realized how important that shopping trip was for me.

Slowly over time, paying bills on time, trying not to overextend myself, asking for help with a grateful heart for specific things from family and friends, I have reached a point where I can see daylight! I now have credit cards. Last year I refinanced my home and I even have a retirement plan!

Credit Tips

- Talk to your creditors. Be up front about problems you may be facing.
- Offer your creditors a pay-off plan, then stick to it, or call them before they call you if the plan fails.
- Shop with a list and stick to it!
- Set a dollar amount for all purchases, including gifts, groceries, gas, and clothing. Don't forget to include them in your budget. These variables are places we sometimes try to really cut corners and then fail to follow through.
- Be up front with your children and other family members. In order for a budget to work, everyone needs to be on the same page and understand the situation.
- Don't be afraid to seek help from other sources. Those resources are there to help and will appreciate you working

hard to overcome your problems. According to my sources in social services, the majority of people using these services use them only an average of two years to overcome difficult situations.

• Coupons are wonderful for a product you need, will use and can afford. But only under those conditions.

• Consider volunteering to help you build references, recommendations, work experiences or any skills you might have a difficult time being paid for in the beginning. You might enjoy it or even find a new career! You will make great contacts and good friends!

• Consider bartering. Do you know someone who sews and who might appreciate a babysitter, housecleaner, or closet organizer?

Chapter Ten

America, the Blending of Many Cultures and Gifts

૨**ૐ**ૐ**ૐ**ૐ

We have worked with women from many different cultures at *Ready for Success.* Our volunteers are also from a variety of cultures and ethnic backgrounds. In America, the globalization of business, the expansion of a multi-cultural, multi-racial workforce has broadened the acceptance of ethnic diversity in clothing in many companies. Not only in this country but also worldwide, the diversity of dress around the world is actually melting into a few limitations of business dress, although traditional business attire is sometimes more "westernized" than other forms of dressing within the same country. The "business casual" dress world has opened up, recognized and allowed for the need for more personal choices. Today many women wish to keep the clothing and customs of their native lands. Yet I have also met numerous women from other countries who tell me they want to dress more "American."

There have always been religious sects within our culture who require the women to dress more modestly than most other Americans. These differences have become less obvious with the freedom of choice the "business casual" world has brought. Even as the pendulum swings to a more professional look, their choice of skirts rather than pants, and longer skirts rather than short skirts, makes their personalized dress less noticeable.

Some cultures expect a woman to be fully covered, exposing only her eyes. That extreme dressing form is difficult for some Americans to accept. To many women and men it represents the repression of women. This angers our sense of what is acceptable but that is not necessarily true for the woman herself in that very traditional dress. At the less radical end of the spectrum we find long skirts, long sleeves, and headscarves *(hajib)* that meet religious and political expectations are easier to accept by our culture in general.

At *Ready for Success* we noticed that some refugees and immigrants have a very strong sense of fabric and clothing construction. They are sometimes appalled with our "business casual" world.

Dressing More "American"

When women from other cultures tell me they want to dress more "American" yet stay within the confines of their sense of their cultural appropriateness, here are some suggestions I offer:

- Americans have a strong sense of what colors go together and what is appropriate for combinations of prints, stripes and plaids. Other cultures select combinations we see as odd. I will suggest to the woman if she wants to look more "American," perhaps we could mix another combination but only if she wants to.
- What are the limits of their dress code? Some of our women will accept skirts slightly above the ankle if they have short

boot shoes that hide their ankles. Some will accept short sleeves or no sleeves if there is some type of blouse or jacket worn over it.

- Sometimes the challenge of working with women from other cultures is to get them to relax a little bit about clothing options.
- Sometimes it is overcoming cultural training of their body language that in this country is misunderstood: not smiling, downcast eyes, and the limp handshake.

As with all of us, what is beautiful is answered by our experiences, our culture and our personal choices. In some African-American groups a well-rounded derrière is considered beautiful, so a tight skirt or pant is more acceptable.

Dressing more "American" has been a great equalizer for immigrants and refugees throughout our history. It certainly helps women assimilate quickly into our culture. We also have an equally long tradition of accepting other modes of dress (older European styles worn by some Amish and Jewish sects, those from India who wear the sari, etc.). Fortunately there is room for both in America. Modesty, cleanliness, and attractiveness are more important criteria in any form of dress.

ॐ

epilogue

ह

I can't tell you for sure how I knew a navy blue blazer would change my life but it did! And that blazer changed the lives of others...

I was blessed to work with "Susan" on all three of her visits. The first was a cold January day. She had just finished a data entry course and was preparing for a job interview in the next week. She was tall, Ruben*esque,* on public assistance and the mother of three children. We talked about working, dressing for the workplace, even dressing everyday in an appropriate manner and paying attention to what her female supervisors wore. "Susan" got her job and revisited us on a hot day in June for summer wardrobe pieces. She said it was a lot of work to work! We all had a good laugh. But she was enjoying it and was pleased with her job—and mostly with herself. In December she came back for a third and final visit. Pulling me aside she said, "Joyce, I was called in to the supervisor this morning. I was so nervous thinking about all the negative things that could happen; getting laid off at Christmas, getting fired! Instead I was told they would be starting a new position in January paying twice my current salary and they would like me to apply for it! Do you know what this means to me? One year ago I thought I would be a poor, single mother forever—one more name on the welfare rolls for the rest of my life! Now I know I am more and my children even treat me differently."

I didn't start out to change anyone's life except my own. I have learned that as I have presented myself differently to the world by the way I dress, the world has responded to me differently. As people came to expect and see me as a confident, capable woman, I began to see myself that way too. Don't get me wrong. I still have those nasty little gremlins occasionally running around in my head saying, *"Who do think you are? And who are you trying to impress?"* But today they are quieter and more respectful in their tone.

As I completed this book, Multiple Sclerosis reared its ugly head and once again forced me to re-examine my life with its challenges and limitations. I retired from the *Ready for Success* program in January of 2004. The seven years with this organization has been an amazing journey. I have been blessed to work with incredible women both as volunteers and clients. I love speaking to groups about dressing for the workplace. Writing this book has been an astonishing experience. So while my time with *Ready for Success* has ended, I don't think God is through with me yet. I look forward to doing what I have been doing, only with a wider audience—that is sharing with other women the confidence, power and strength we can present through our personal appearance.

On a more personal note, I am married to a wonderful man. I did a much better job of choosing a partner this time! Life is good—that is not to say perfect. Few people have the opportunity to look at their life and say, "That was hard but now I know why."

It seems like many, many years ago when I leaned against the shower wall and cried, *"Please God, help me out of this craziness. What do you want me to do?"* I hope I'm doing it.

— *Joyce*

❧

18 Success Secrets

by Joyce Nelson Shellhart

#1

Shopping and spending are two different activities. Your bank account is not checked before you walk in the door of any store.

#2

Sometimes our closest family and friends have the most trouble with our new look. We no longer fit their image of us. Ask yourself, who do you need to impress? Start with yourself. *(Yes, you matter!)*

#3

Just as you would not consider wearing your McDonald's uniform out on a date, the clothes you wear to work are not what you will probably wear out with your friends or around the house. It is what you need to gain positive strokes at work.

#4

Choose a base color to work with. Black is probably the easiest and looks great on most women. *(In hindsight I should have chosen black over navy blue when I began.)*

#5

How can you sell yourself, if you don't think you have anything to sell? You are worth this opportunity. Repeat this to yourself as often as is necessary.

#6

Almost everyone who has ever accepted a job or promotion thinks, *"This is over my head and sooner or later they will find out that I don't really know what I am doing."* Never let fear stop you from taking on a new challenge.

#7

Dress for your workplace. You are representing your employer by how you dress and present yourself—not your eligibility on the dating circuit.

#8

Start wearing scarfs. There is no real secret to wearing a scarf. Put it on. Decide what feels comfortable to you. Then carry it off with attitude! No fussing or fidgeting allowed!

#9
Wear appropriate shoes. Other women may admire a cute open-toed shoe with a lovely pedicure but many men will view that attention to your feet as frivolous or your trying to look sexy. Is that how you want to be viewed in your workplace?

#10
Shoes last longer with regular polishing and rotating their use! Well-tended shoes say a lot about your attention to detail and concern about your appearance.

#11
Pay attention to the details of your personal appearance. Whether you work in a very professional setting or a more casual setting, the details are important.

12
Learn to shake hands–firmly–positively! It is an important first impression. Many employers will judge you by your handshake.

#13
SMILE. Your smile is the most important thing you will put on for your interview and job! If you are not comfortable smiling around strangers, practice!

#14
Never put a tattoo where it can be seen in an interview.

#15
I have yet to meet a woman who thinks she has the perfect body whether she is size 6, 12, 16, or 24. We waste too much time and energy obsessing about our bodies! Remember the ads with supermodels are even retouched! Let's move on ladies

#16
Hang the pieces to your suits separately. You will see them as separates with more choices of clothing partners within your closet.

#17
Don't buy it, no matter how great the deal is, if: • *it is the wrong size today even if you are on a diet* • *the color isn't good on you* • *it is the right size but poor fit for your body type* • *it needs alterations, unless the store offers them for free, or you do that type of thing regularly (don't just add it to your pile to do someday)* • *it is still more than your budget allows unless you will wear it enough times to justify the cost.*

#18
Sometimes a sale or bargain is not one! Do the math of a sale.